THE SIMULARITY PROPOSITION

An Informal Essay on Tech, Reality and Contemporary Theoretical Perspectives in Physics, Artificial Intelligence & Philosophy

ANTHONY HORTON

TABLE OF CONTENTS

Part Three: Simularity - the Intersection of The Singularity and The Simulation Hypothesis   47

Part Four: The Crossroads of Religious Faith, Spirituality and The Simularity   67

Part Five: The Final Synthesis - Concluding Observations   81

References   85

Introduction

The Simularity Proposition

The subtitle was probably the 'hook' that has you reading this first part: *An Essay on Tech, Reality and Contemporary Theoretical Perspectives in Physics, Artificial Intelligence & Philosophy* - I know, it's quite catchy, eh?

Here is what the essay is actually all about: in the evolving domain of modern intellectual thought, there are two relatively recent contributions and transformative theories that stand at the forefront: The Singularity and The Simulation Hypothesis. These concepts, each individually thought-provoking on their own merits, offer compelling insights into the fundamental questions of human existence, the future of technology and even the structures of our reality. When we consider these two theories together, however, they lead us to a set of possibilities that transcend their individual qualities. Through this integration of ideas, we can start to conceive a persuasive and comprehensive theory of the universe. This essay, at its core, is about those possibilities.

Although it is not the most creative terminology to describe the combination of these two ideas, I've landed on the term 'Simularity'. As I've committed sentences and paragraphs to describing it in written form, my spellcheck continuously reminds me that 'simularity' is not (yet!) an actual word. Eventually, it dawned on me that it was too simplistic – simply fusing the main words together – so I extended it to The Simulation Proposition. If anything, it makes it sound a little fancier.

The Simularity Proposition, for some, will seem to be an 'out there' idea (although, as you read on, *what and where* 'out there' actually is, may not be *what and where* we tend to think it is). In order for it to be a compelling idea, first, we have to agree that we, as modern humans, are on the brink of a convergence between our consciousness and advanced technology. This suggests that we also must collectively agree that we are closing in on a stage in our development as a species where the margins between reality and technology are not-so-gradually being blurred into indistinction.

I confess, none of the ideas contained in this essay can be considered original thought on my part. They are notions and thinking borne from the philosophies, discoveries and hypotheses of those who possess intellectual capacities far beyond anything I have or will ever achieve.

I will also note that this essay should not, in any manner, be construed as an academic paper or a scholarly undertaking. The joy of being able to write about random subjects that interest you, for the pure gratification of getting all these admittedly odd and convoluted ideas out of you head and into a format that seems sensible, is a luxury reserved for those of us who have reached the end zone when it comes to formal academic pursuits. So, to any reader with pedantic tendencies, I apologize in advance for not following the rigorous standards of citation, formatting and all the other various rules and requirements for academic essays. No one is marking this and I'm not looking for an advanced degree in whatever bizarre discipline this subject might qualify for – so I just skipped the mind-numbing, nit-picky activities and interjected some deviant informality here and there. I have, however, cited quotes and ideas from the many experts whose brilliance I've relied on so that I am giving them due and proper credit and, similarly, I have provided references of all content I've quoted and/or studied in researching specific topics.

The content presented here represents the culmination of concepts and ideas I've been reading about for roughly two decades. It started with Ray Kurzweil. When I first read *The Singularity* roughly seventeen years ago, it literally – and mind-blowingly – had a profound impact on how I viewed the world and the future. And given that most of what Kurzweil predicted back then has essentially come to be our reality in 2024, I assume I picked a robust and solid hypothesis to follow. I've always been an early adopter of technology and have been keenly attuned to advancements in networking and information technology since the late nineties. In the endless cycle of 'one-thing-leading-to-another', these interests led to years of reading a wide range of material; from history, to technology, to quantum physics, to consciousness studies, to world religions, bridging these back to theories like singularity and simulation and, ultimately, back to what I can only describe as good old philosophy. I am not an expert in any of these areas – my doctorate is in business administration and, other than a few references to macroeconomic considerations, this subject has nothing to do with business. (My wife insisted on using the 'Dr' prefix which I tend to avoid because she said it gives my non-fiction writing a more credibility). What this all means is that the proceeding content is merely a layperson's view, mingling several ideas together into what, hopefully, is an interesting proposition.

It begins through the process of mixing the principles of The Singularity, as articulated by Ray Kurzweil, stirring them a bowl with the provocative assertions of The Simulation Hypothesis, championed by Rizwan Virk and Nick Bostrom. In doing so, I've tried to create the *mis en place* for the dish that is The Simularity Proposition. It is intended to lead to a palatable dish which represents a conceivable explanation for the trajectory of human evolution, nature of existence and possible destiny for our species. It is intended mainly to make us question today's interpretations of our emergent experience. The beliefs that govern our perceptions become less convincing in the light of The Simularity Proposition, which not only addresses the logical and philosophical gaps inherent in traditional existential beliefs, but also provides a convincing scientific basis for understanding consciousness, existence and the universe.

It's hard to put Ray Kurzweil into a category. Is he a scholar, a technologist or a futurist? My take would be, 'all of the above'. Kurzweil has received well-earned acclaim for his predictive accuracy and through-provoking ideas on how our species will inevitably evolve. As noted by Kevin Kelly, founding executive editor of Wired, "Kurzweil's genius lies in his ability to foresee the integration of human and machine, predicting not just the next step but the next leap in technological evolution" (Kelly, 2005). I have to admit, having read and digested Kurzweil's ideas for the past 6,337 or so days (adjusted for leap years), I find his reasoning to be as close to irrefutable as possible. Particularly as his prognostications continue to morph into our reality year after year.

Similarly, Rizwan Virk's exploration of The Simulation Hypothesis has garnered attention for its provocative approach. At first, the proposal that we may all exist in a sophisticated simulation comes across as impractical and improbable. Yet, once you accept that our knowledge of the universe is at an early stage in its development and consider the dots this MIT-educated, video game expert connects in supporting its plausibility, we can't help but hesitate to challenge our understanding of our reality. David Chalmers, a prominent philosopher and cognitive scientist, commented that "Virk's hypothesis challenges us to reconsider our understanding of reality, merging ancient philosophical questions with cutting-edge technology and quantum physics" (Chalmers, 2016). And it also causes me to constantly scrutinize my fellow humans whenever I'm in public and attempt to figure out who the NPC's are (an inside joke for any gamers out there who, for some inexplicable reason, first found this weird little essay of mine and then found themselves, even more inexplicably, reading it!).

The Singularity and The Simulation Hypothesis: An Intersection

Time to get serious and discuss what comes next. We will explore the thinking behind The Singularity and The Simulation Hypothesis extensively since these concepts form the foundation of The Simularity Proposition (there goes spellcheck again – a consistent red line under *Simularity* whenever I type it). The Singularity is a concept popularized by Kurzweil in what is probably his most famous book, *The Singularity Is Near*. At the time of this writing, he is due to release his latest, *The Singularity Is Nearer*, in June 2024. I have been eagerly awaiting the new revelations and updates that will undoubtedly be articulated in this new publication.

Kurzweil's body of thought envisions a future where the exponential growth of technology leads to a point of unprecedented transformation. According to Kurzweil, this future, which is often referred to as the Technological Singularity, will occur when artificial intelligence surpasses human intelligence. At this point of singularity, we will experience both acute and irreversible changes to civilization. His writing is characterized by the Law of Accelerating Returns, which suggests that the pace of technological progress is not linear but exponential, with each advancement building upon previous innovations at an increasingly rapid rate, driven by deepening computational capacity and the ability of AI to leverage the full spectrum of knowledge we are constantly advancing on the back of this technology explosion.

Kurzweil forecasts that by the mid-21st century, humans will necessarily merge with technology in a seamless and symbiotic relationship.

This convergence is expected to empower us with the ability to transcend our biological limitations, enhance our cognitive competencies and significantly extend our lifespans – perhaps even indefinitely. The Singularity will bring about a new era of superintelligence, where machines possess the ability to think, reason and solve complex problems beyond the capacity of the human mind. This transformation will redefine what it means to be human, as we integrate ourselves with artificial intelligence, nanotechnology and other emerging technological and knowledge-based advancements.

In *The Singularity Is Near*, Kurzweil states, "We will become the intelligence of the universe, and we will extend our reach beyond the limits of biology and our planet" (Kurzweil, 2005). And Kurzweil isn't alone. This vision of the future has been supported by many in the scientific community. Peter Diamandis, founder of the X Prize Foundation, remarks that, "Kurzweil's predictions are not only plausible but also inevitable given the current trajectory of technological advancement" (Diamandis, 2011).

It is this inevitability that struck me when I first read *The Singularity Is Near*. We not only have evidence of this hastened build towards a merging of biology and technology, the way Kurzweil presents his case, tracing back our unique evolutionary history of developing and exploiting tools, along with the more recent phenomenon of expanding computer capabilities as a man-made instrument, leads students like me to the conclusion that we are unalterably on the path her foretells.

Key Components of The Singularity

While it seems almost like sacrilege to sort the main principles of The Singularity into short summary precis, it's necessary for what comes next in the essay, so here goes:

Exponential Growth of Computing Power: The doubling of computational capacity approximately every two years, as described by Moore's Law, is a cornerstone of The Singularity. The rapid increase in processing power we have already witnessed in our lifetimes will enable the development of highly advanced AI systems capable of performing tasks that were previously unimaginable. The implications of this exponential curve will ultimately extend well beyond mere computational function; they also acknowledge the potential for AI to surpass human intelligence and achieve superintelligence, fundamentally altering our current day comprehension of knowledge and problem-solving.

Merging of Humans and Technology: Through innovations such as brain-computer interfaces, neural implants and biotechnology, humans will enhance their cognitive and physical abilities leading to a new and transformative form of augmented existence. This merger will not only increase our capabilities as individuals but it is predicted that it will also manifest into a collective intelligence, where human minds and machines exist together and interact effortlessly. The potential benefits that may be derived because of this symbiosis are considerable, ranging from instant recall memory, real-time learning or accessing of information, to physical augmentations that extend human abilities beyond our biological limitations.

Implications for Human Evolution: The Singularity will also entail a significant leap in the evolution of humanity as we transition from purely biological organisms to hybrid forms that will conjoin both organic and synthetic components. This evolution will be driven by our ability to manipulate and enhance our own biology and is anticipated to lead to the emergence of a new species that transcends traditional human constraints. The Singularity will cause us to test our understanding of what it means to be human and force us to reconsider the ethical and philosophical implications of such advancements.

Ethical and Philosophical Considerations: The rise of superintelligent machines raises important questions about the nature of consciousness, identity and the moral implications of humans producing entities that will, in all likelihood, surpass human intelligence as we have experienced it. These considerations include the risks we've all been presented with recently when it comes to AI, such as loss of control, ethical treatment of intelligent machines and the societal impact of widespread automation and machine learning. The Singularity will require a reexamination of our ethical frameworks and a commitment to ensuring that technological advancements are aligned with human values and well-being. Ironically, it will also require us to evaluate the efficacy of our value systems and consider new ones.

It is an irremediable truth that, by the time I have published this essay, the Law of Accelerating Returns warrants that technology, computational function and knowledge will quickly expand to make some of the data points and reflections outdated if not instantaneously archaic!

The Simulation Hypothesis is a thought-provoking theory articulated by Rizwan Virk who proposes that our reality is, in fact, a sophisticated simulation, most likely one that was created by an advanced civilization. My own thinking is that any supposition around the origins of such a simulation invariably result in an infinite logic loop, since our awareness of history of this universe and existence is limited to this very universe and existence, leaving open a limitless canvas of possibilities. Drawing on concepts from quantum mechanics, superposition and the multiverse theory, Virk lays out the argument that what we perceive as the physical world around is, in fact, a digital construct, not unlike highly advanced computer simulations we experience today, although primitive in comparison.

I know, it seems too much like science fiction to be taken seriously, right? When we consider the premise, however, with Virk's supporting concepts, it begins to take shape as a distinct possibility. The hypothesis is rooted in the observation that the universe operates with extraordinary precision and mathematical consistency. This is not dissimilar to the code that underpins a computer program. In addition, quantum mechanics, with its perplexing and counterintuitive occurrences such as particle-wave duality and entanglement, provides a framework for understanding how a simulated reality might actually work. According to Virk and another brilliant simulation proponent, Nick Bostrom, the seemingly random and probabilistic nature of quantum events can be explained by the underlying algorithms that serve to govern this simulation.

David Chalmers noted, "Virk's hypothesis challenges us to reconsider our understanding of reality, merging ancient philosophical questions with cutting-edge technology and quantum physics" (Chalmers, 2016). This thought-provoking approach has also been echoed by Max Tegmark, a renowned physicist, who stated, "The Simulation Hypothesis offers a fresh perspective on the nature of reality, inviting us to explore the boundaries of science and philosophy" (Tegmark, 2018).

If we also consider how we have only scratched the service in our knowledge of the universe and, by extension, our perceived reality within it, the idea that our physical world is simply comprised of digital renderings becomes at least within the boundaries of the credible.

Key Components of The Simulation Hypothesis

Quantum Mechanics and Superposition: The principles of quantum mechanics, particularly the idea that particles can exist in multiple states simultaneously (superposition), provide key support for the idea that our reality is something produced by complex computational processes. The phenomena of superposition suggests that the fabric of reality is not fixed but is created by a dynamic and programmable system that is subject to the rules and logic inherent within a sophisticated simulation. The possible implications of this are, of course, profound. The idea directly challenges our current understanding of reality and suggests that our universe may be more like a computer program than a physical construct.

The Role of Technology in Simulation: As our own technology advances, particularly when it comes to more recent developments like virtual reality (VR) and artificial intelligence (AI), it becomes increasingly conceivable that an advanced civilization, consciousness or 'thing we can't comprehend' could create a simulated universe indistinguishable from our own. The advancements of immersive VR experiences and sophisticated AI systems provide demonstrable evidence of the potential for creating detailed and interactive simulations, supporting the idea that our reality could be the product of such a technology. Of course, this leads to all sorts of mind-bending questions about the nature of the creators of our simulation and their intentions. Nonetheless, is it so different from the questions that come up when considering our collective human habit of conjuring up deities that supposedly created us and govern our existence?

Multiverse Theory: The idea that multiple, parallel universes exist simultaneously also aligns with the hypothesis of a simulated reality. Within this context, it becomes possible that different simulations or even different instances of the same simulation could run concurrently. This multiverse perspective implies that our universe exists as just one instance of what could be many possible realities, each governed by its own set of instructions and parameters. The existence of parallel simulations could explain many of the anomalies and mysteries observed in our own experience (including things as far along the weirdness continuum as unexplained paranormal phenomenon to the commonplace experience of *déjà vu*) while also providing an explanation for the complexity and diversity of reality.

Philosophical Implications: The Simulation Hypothesis challenges our understanding of reality, consciousness and the nature of existence, prompting profound existential queries about the purpose and meaning of life. If our reality is, in fact, a massive and complicated simulation it requires us to think more about the nature of our consciousness and the existence of free will. Could we or some of those we interact with be part of a sophisticated game, or do we possess genuine autonomy and self-awareness? The implications of this hypothesis extend to our understanding of identity, purpose and the nature of our perceptions of reality itself.

The Singularity and The Simulation Hypothesis provide an intersection point, from which we can explore a unique and sometimes perplexing but also transformative point of view on the true nature of reality and human existence. While both theories provide valuable insights on their own, their combined implications become far-reaching and insightful. The Simularity Proposition advances the idea that the convergence of these two streams of reasoning can lead to a comprehensive set of thought-provoking ideas regarding our place in the universe and the ultimate trajectory of human evolution.

The Simularity Proposition draws on multiple disciplines including philosophy, quantum physics, artificial intelligence, modern technology, history and evolution. By integrating these diverse fields, we can develop a holistic background that contemplates the elemental questions of existence and consciousness. This interdisciplinary approach, incorporating both historical and contemporary thoughts and facts, sets us up to explore the connections between seemingly disparate areas of study and look to uncover the deeper principles that govern our reality. The combination of The Singularity and The Simulation Hypothesis not only provides us with an interesting set of possible explanations for the human experience, memory and mortality, it also suggests that our reality may be a product of advanced technology and a steppingstone towards a higher level of existence. The notion that we are part of a sophisticated simulation implies that our lives have a purpose and design beyond mere biological survival. This perspective can offer new understanding into the nature of consciousness and the ultimate destiny of humanity – if we do actually have a prescribed or intended destiny at all.

It would be tempting to put forward a theory such as The Simularity Proposition without fully addressing some of the seemingly logical and philosophical gaps it inevitably elicits. I intend to tackle these tough questions as they relate to the full weight of what I am postulating in the following pages. Traditional religious and existential thought often appear to struggle when it comes to reconciling the spiritual and metaphysical aspects of human existence with the logical and scientific principles that govern the universe. The Simularity Proposition bridges this gap by offering a logical and scientifically grounded explanation for the mysteries of consciousness and reality. By combining the insights of The Singularity and The Simulation Hypothesis, we can develop a philosophical structure that unifies the spiritual and material dimensions of reality.

Sounds a bit nuts, right? Read on.

The Simularity Proposition is not all sunshine and roses. It raises important ethical and philosophical questions about the nature of reality, the responsibilities of advanced civilizations and the potential consequences of creating superintelligent machines. It challenges us to consider the moral implications of our technological advancements and the impact they will have on future generations. By exploring these questions, we can develop a more nuanced and ethical approach to the development and deployment of advanced technologies.

From the most optimistic perspective, the insights gained from The Simularity Proposition can inform a wide range of practical applications, from the development of advanced AI systems to the exploration of virtual reality and the potential for creating new simulations. By understanding the underlying principles of our own, possibly simulated, reality, we can harness the power of technology to enhance human capabilities and improve overall quality of life. This includes advancements in healthcare, education, entertainment and other areas where technology can have a transformative impact.

The future envisioned by The Simularity Proposition is one where humans are no longer bound by the constraints of their biological form. Instead, we will have the ability to enhance and transform ourselves through technology, achieving levels of intelligence and capability that are currently beyond our comprehension. This future holds the promise of solving some of humanity's most pressing challenges, from disease and aging to environmental degradation and social inequality.

In the sections that follow, we will delve deeper into the key components of The Singularity and The Simulation Hypothesis, explore the interdisciplinary connections between these theories and examine a range of ethical, philosophical and practical implications of The Simularity Proposition.

PART ONE

The Singularity

Overview of The Singularity

The idea of The Singularity has been developed, expanded and made popular by futurist Ray Kurzweil. The concept itself originates from the realm of science fiction along with some of the ideas put forth by early technologists. The term 'singularity' was initially introduced in this context by science fiction author and mathematician Vernor Vinge in his 1993 piece "The Coming Technological Singularity", where he speculated that "we will soon create intelligences superior to our own leading to a point in history akin to a singularity, an intellectual shift as incomprehensible as the twisted space time at the heart of a black hole propelling us beyond our current understanding" (Vinge, 1993). Vinge's depiction of The Singularity is based on advancements in computing power and artificial intelligence leading to a future where technological progress surpasses the limitations of biology.

Expanding on Vinge's ideas, Kurzweil has elevated the concept into a compelling theory of technological development. Kurzweil, in his book *The Singularity Is Near; When Humans Transcend Biology* discusses the concept of the Law of Accelerating Returns, which suggests that the pace of change in evolutionary systems, such as technological advancements, tends to grow exponentially over time. The idea of this process has roots dating back several decades, notably highlighted by Gordon Moore's observation in 1965 and now known as Moore's Law. Moore's Law states that the number of transistors on a microchip doubles approximately every two years. Kurzweil emphasizes that Moore's Law is one aspect of the principle of the Law of Accelerating Returns.

The Law of Accelerating Returns can also be linked back to theories proposed by figures like Alan Turing. Turing, recognized as a pioneer in computer science, laid down the groundwork for understanding both the capabilities and limitations of computing machines. In his paper from 1950 titled "Computing Machinery and Intelligence", Turing explored the idea of machines simulating intelligence, a concept that has had a lasting impact on AI research. What sets Kurzweil's work apart is its integration of established theories and its depiction of humanity's development which has led us to our current technology-driven, post-industrial era.

Several foundational concepts within The Singularity draw inspiration from Charles Darwin's theory of evolution. In *On the Origin of Species*, Darwin discusses how species within a genus often exhibit similarities in behavior, constitution and structure leading to competition when they interact. This notion of evolution is akin to Kurzweil's belief that technological entities, like species, will evolve through natural selection processes resulting in more advanced forms of intelligence. Kevin Kelly, the editor of *Wired* magazine has highlighted the rapid growth of technology in his book *What Technology Wants*, Kelly explains how technology advances similarly to living organisms, driven by an inclination towards increased complexity and effectiveness. According to him technology follows its course resembling the paths seen in biological life (Kelly, 2010).

The Singularity encompasses ideas that depict a future where artificial intelligence surpasses human intelligence causing significant societal changes. One crucial aspect is the growth of computing power as outlined by Moore's Law. This exponential increase in capability fuels the conditions leading up to The Singularity. This growth accelerates over time driving rapid advancements in AI and other technologies and ultimately fostering exponential growth in knowledge and computational capacity.

The convergence of biology with technology is a key concept in The Singularity. This involves the development of brain computer interfaces, smart nanotechnologies, neural implants and biotechnological enhancements that enhance our human abilities. Kurzweil envisions a world where our species can improve its physical and cognitive skills by merging with the technology they create.

Another significant aspect of The Singularity is the creation of superintelligent machines. These AI machines will be able to solve problems, generate knowledge and potentially exhibit consciousness. Nick Bostrom's book *Superintelligence; Paths, Dangers, Strategies* delves into the routes to achieving superintelligence and examines the existential risks associated with it. What is fascinating is how, in 2024 we are witnessing rapid stages of AI development that make it difficult to argue that we are not paving the way towards superintelligence.

With the emergence of AI, profound ethical and philosophical dilemmas come to light. Questions regarding the rights of AI entities, the risks associated with human control loss and the societal implications of automation become crucial focal points. Philosopher David Chalmers emphasizes that the rise of superintelligent AI could herald a moment in history that sparks inquiries into identity, consciousness and even the essence of reality – something we'll dive into in more detail when we cover simulation theory.

Various scholars and technologists have lent support to Kurzweil's predictions and theories. For instance, robotics and AI trailblazer Hans Moravec has combed through the landscape of machines in his work *Mind Children; The Future of Robot and Human Intelligence.* Moravec envisions a future where robots will evolve to match or even surpass human thresholds of intelligence, obfuscating the boundaries between humans and machines. Likewise, computer scientist and futurist Jaron Lanier offers insights in his book *You Are Not a Gadget* recognizing AI's potential while also sounding a note of caution against dependence on technology. Lanier stresses that as intelligent machines continue to progress it is vital to safeguard values and creativity from being overshadowed by automated processes.

Despite receiving interest and backing from leading thinkers and forward-thinking intellectuals, The Singularity has encountered obstacles and criticisms from various quarters. One of the criticisms comes from cognitive scientist Gary Marcus, who contends that current AI technologies are still far from achieving genuine general intelligence. In his piece "The Challenges of AI" Marcus points out: "Despite progress modern AI systems lack the adaptability and overall problem-solving capabilities that define intelligence. The path to superintelligence is riddled with technical hurdles that are frequently underestimated" (Marcus, 2018). However, it is also worth noting that this perspective was shared in 2018 before the emergence of large language models that now routinely perform data analysis and problem-solving functions.

Philosopher John Searle has raised doubts about the concept of superintelligent AI by asserting that machines, regardless of their proficiency, cannot possess understanding or consciousness. In his well-known Chinese Room argument Searle suggests that "a machine might mimic human responses but lacks genuine comprehension of the information it processes. True consciousness necessitates more than symbol manipulation" (Searle, 1980).

In response to these challenges, supporters of The Singularity such as Kurzweil have put forward rebuttals. Addressing Marcus' concerns,

Kurzweil acknowledges the limitations of AI while highlighting the pace of technological advancements that we have all witnessed in our daily lives. He suggests that despite the existing constraints of today's AI systems, progress is accelerating. Breakthroughs in fields such as networking, quantum computing and brain machine interfaces will bring us closer to achieving general intelligence (Kurzweil, 2005).

Regarding Searle's criticism, Kurzweil and other advocates of The Singularity argue that the development of consciousness in machines fundamentally hinges on complexity and computational potential. According to Kurzweil in *How to Create a Mind: The Secret of Human Thought Revealed,* consciousness is a property that results from the neural networks in the brain. By replicating and surpassing this level of complexity in machines it is feasible that they too may evolve into different and new forms of consciousness (Kurzweil, 2012).

Another noteworthy viewpoint is presented by physicist and complexity scientist, Geoffrey West who has studied the growth patterns of social systems. In his book *Scale; The Universal Laws of Growth, Innovation, Sustainability and the Pace of Life, in Organisms, Cities, Economies and Companies,* West argues that rapid growth often proves unsustainable and may result in collapse. He emphasizes the idea that exponential growth encounters resource constraints and other obstacles over time. West stresses the importance of acknowledging these limitations and promoting practices in technology and economic advancement. In contrast, Kurzweil acknowledges that perpetual exponential growth is not feasible within a system but contends that technological systems are dynamic and can surpass their boundaries through innovation and paradigm shifts. He highlights how each stage of evolution introduces capabilities that address previous limitations. Kurzweil cites instances where technological shifts have surmounted constraints. For example, the transition from vacuum tubes to transistors and later to circuits enabled exponential advancements in computing power despite initial limitations. Developments in quantum computing and nanotechnology offer avenues for exponential growth.

The idea of 'singularities' across multiple fields implies that when one area reaches its limits a new field might emerge to sustain the trend of rapid growth. For instance, the fusion of biotechnology and information technology could result in innovations in medicine, synthetic biology and the enhancement of human capabilities. Recent progress in neuroscience and cognitive science seems to lend support to the notion of machine consciousness, as if validating Kurzweil's predictions. Through innovations in technology that allow for in-depth brain research, we are uncovering similarities between our neural processes and machine-like functions. Neuroscientist Giulio Tononi's work on Integrated Information Theory (IIT) suggests that consciousness stems from information integration within a system. Tononi proposes that as AI systems become more intricate and interconnected, they may exhibit these same properties (Tononi, 2015).

So, we've now established that the concept of The Singularity envisions a future where rapid technological growth brings about changes in society and the nature of intelligence. Let's take a look more specifically at some of the evidence supporting the viability of Kurzweil's predictions.

Empirical Evidence and Examples

Evidence from several fields of study supports the idea of exponential technology growth. A prime example is the Internet, which virtually every one of us on Earth is familiar with. Since its inception, the Internet has grown precipitously, with the number of devices and users doubling about every five years. This growth has been fueled by advancements in computing capacity, the expansion of network infrastructure and digital technologies. As Kurzweil points out "The internet illustrates how technology grows exponentially. It has changed our world in a few decades. Its impact continues to speed up" (Kurzweil, 2005).

In biotechnology the cost of sequencing the genome has plummeted since the Human Genome Project's completion in 2003. The cost has decreased from around $100 million in 2003 to less than $1,000 today following a trend similar to Moore's Law (National Human Genome Research Institute, 2020). This significant cost reduction has opened research and application opportunities for information transforming fields like personalized medicine and genetic engineering.

In his book *The Age of Em; Work, Love and Life when Robots Rule the Earth*, economist Robin Hanson jumps into how the rapid increase in computing power will pave the way for AI systems known as 'ems' that will reshape both the economy and society. According to Hanson, the exponential growth in capacity will result in the emergence of emulations that will bring about changes to work dynamics, relationships and economic structures.

The emergence of deep learning algorithms like convolutional neural networks (CNNs) and generative adversarial networks (GANs) has led to breakthroughs in tasks such as image recognition and translation, natural language processing and autonomous systems. These advancements have been driven by an expansive rise in data accessibility and computational capabilities alongside enhancements in AI models and methodologies.

The increase in computing power is evident across many sectors and applications, with microprocessor development standing out as one of the most notable examples. Since the debut of the microprocessor, the Intel 4004 in 1971, we've seen a surge in the number of transistors packed onto a single chip. From 2,300 then to an astounding 50 billion in today's processors. This rapid growth has resulted in massive strides in computing speed, energy efficiency and hardware size reduction.

Another compelling illustration lies in the realm of intelligence and machine learning. The exponential rise in capabilities has fueled the creation of AI models like deep neural networks that excel at tackling intricate tasks with precision and speed. Take, for instance GPT-3 (Generative Pre-trained Transformer 3) developed by OpenAI boasting

175 billion parameters within the adjustable weights of its neural network and making it one of the most extensive and potent large language models ever created. Such advancements owe their existence to the surge in computing power that facilitates training and deploying intricate algorithms.

Looking ahead to quantum computing projections we can also expect speedy progress on this frontier. Quantum computers harness quantum mechanics principles to execute computations beyond the restrictions of a computer's capabilities. Leading players such as IBM, Google and Rigetti are spearheading efforts to craft quantum processors capable of solving problems exponentially faster than traditional computers. For example, Google's quantum processor, known as Sycamore, made an achievement in 2019 by completing a computation in 200 seconds that would have taken the most powerful supercomputer in the world around 10,000 years to do.

Renowned theoretical physicist Michio Kaku has discussed how quantum computing stands on the brink of transforming industrial sectors. In his book, *The Future of the Mind: The Scientific Quest to Understand, Enhance, and Empower the Mind,* Kaku explores the potential of quantum computers that utilize quantum mechanics principles to process information in ways beyond classical computer capabilities. By harnessing qubits that can exist in states simultaneously, quantum computers can conduct calculations concurrently, significantly boosting computational power. This new capability has the potential to drive innovation in replicating chemical reactions, which could advance the discovery and creation of drugs as well as enhance energy efficiency in processes such as nitrogen fixation and fusion power generation (Big Think, 2023).

Kaku also highlights that quantum computing will not just boost our capacities but will fundamentally transform industries. He points out that quantum computers can tackle cryptography problems, optimize processes and potentially revolutionize fields like medicine by simulating molecular interactions at a minute level. However, he acknowledges the challenges involved with decoherence', where quantum states are disrupted by external influences (Kaku, 2021). Despite these hurdles Kaku maintains an outlook that quantum computing will eventually outshine computing systems ushering in a new era of technological and scientific advancements.

The rapid growth of computing capabilities has revolutionized data storage and processing. Cloud computing platforms like Amazon Web Services (AWS), Microsoft Azure and Google Cloud have facilitated the handling of unfathomable volumes of data at all levels. Through distributed computing structures and advanced data management technologies these platforms offer incredibly efficient solutions for researchers and users.

Merging of Humans and Technology

Kurzweil paints a picture of a future where humans will enhance their bodies and minds using cutting edge technologies to attain a form of superior intelligence. He foresees that by the 2040's or sooner, non-biological intelligence will surpass intelligence as the dominant form on Earth and seamlessly merging with our own. According to Kurzweil, this integration will make us more non-biological than the humans we have known for all our history (perhaps a good thing in the case of some!).

Kurzweil's future encompasses the advancement of brain computer interfaces (BCI's), neural implants and biotechnological enhancements that will allow interaction between humans and machines to boost both physical and mental abilities. In his vision, he foresees a world where we can store our memories, instantly access information and even alter our emotions and personalities (Kurzweil, 2005). One prominent viewpoint that sides with Kurzweil's forecasts comes from

Elon Musk, the CEO of SpaceX and Tesla who established Neuralink to advance BCI's. While expressing concerns about superintelligent AI's dangers publicly, Musk also sees enhancement as a way to keep up with AI progress. He suggests that forming a relationship with artificial intelligence is essential to tackle AI challenges effectively; "If you can't beat it join it" (Musk, 2017). Cutting edge companies like Neuralink, Kernel and Paradromics are paving the way in developing BCI's. Neural implants represent a technology that merges biology with sophisticated machinery. These implants hold promise in treating conditions, restoring capabilities and boosting cognitive performance. For instance, Cochlear implants have successfully restored hearing for those with hearing impairment while retinal implants are in the works to revive vision for individuals with eye disorders.

Likewise, in his book *Homo Deus; A Brief History of Tomorrow*, historian Yuval Noah Harari poses compelling ideas around humanity's future in the era of biotechnology and artificial intelligence. Harari explores the concept of 'Homo Deus' predicting a species surpassing Homo Sapiens through these advancements. He maintains that the combination of humans and technology will reshape our understanding of humanity empowering us to manage our biology and improve our physical abilities (Harari, 2016). Philosopher and cognitive scientist Andy Clark explores the concept of humans as cyborgs in his book *Natural Born Cyborgs; Minds, Technologies and the Future of Human Intelligence*, proposing that human reliance on tools and technology has always been a part of our existence. Clark suggests that integrating technology with the body and mind is a continuation of this historical trend. He explains how the distinction between humans and machines is blurring as technology becomes integrated into our processes (Clark, 2003).

Recent advancements in fields like engineering and synthetic biology are also instrumental in blending humans with technology. Technologies such as CRISPR (Clustered Regularly Interspaced Short Palindromic Repeats) Cas9 enable manipulation of the genome, offering opportunities to correct genetic disorders and enhance desired traits. Recently, CRISPR technology achieved a significant milestone with the development of a cure for sickle cell anemia. The U.S. Food and Drug Administration (FDA) approved the first-ever CRISPR-based therapy, Casgevy for sickle cell disease (SCD) in December 2023.

This fusion of humans and technology carries implications for individuals by transforming their abilities, experiences and identities. Enhanced cognitive and physical capacities can lead to improved quality of life, heightened productivity levels as well as novel forms of creativity and self-expression. For example, individuals equipped with BCI's may acquire skills swiftly, communicate efficiently and access information instantaneously. In the future imagined by Kurzweil humans could enhance their memory and thinking abilities using implants to process and store large amounts of information. He suggests that connecting our minds directly with computer systems could boost our powers, essentially merging humans with machines (Kurzweil, 2005).

Of course, these developments also give rise to philosophical dilemmas concerning personal identity and autonomy. As people integrate technology into their bodies and minds the line between the 'self' and external devices blurs, prompting reflections that can be unsettling, especially when influenced by films like *The Terminator* and *The Matrix*. These considerations provoke intriguing discussions about consciousness, free will and the continuity of identity. Philosopher David Chalmers suggests that if our minds intertwine closely with our advanced technological tools, we need to rethink what it truly means to be an individual capable of autonomous thought (Chalmers, 2010).

When people start incorporating technologies into their lives, even today, they often undergo shifts in how they perceive themselves and their personal identities. As ethicist Julian Savulescu points out "The psychological implications of enhancement are profound. We need to carefully weigh the potential advantages and drawbacks for individual wellbeing" (Savulescu, 2011). The possibility of improving abilities and enhancing memory could bring about new ways of seeing oneself and expressing one's identity. but it could also pose challenges concerning mental health and overall wellness.

Impacts on Society

Similarly, the potential societal implications concerning the assimilation of humans and technology are profound and multifaceted. Technologically enhanced individuals would assuredly have significant advantages over others in terms of cognitive abilities, physical capabilities and high-speed access to information. This could lead to new, unintended forms of social stratification and inequality; disparities which could exacerbate existing social divisions and create new challenges for social cohesion and justice. As an example, access to enhancement technologies may be limited by economic factors, leading to a society where only the wealthy can afford to participate and have access to the tools and procedures required to augment their abilities. This would give rise to a new class of 'enhanced' individuals who would possess significant advantages over those who cannot access these technologies and, thereby, deepening social and economic inequalities. As Harari illuminates, "The emergence of a new class of superhumans could lead to unprecedented levels of inequality and social division" (Harari, 2016).

On the positive side, the widespread adoption of human enhancement technologies could lead to significant societal benefits, such as increased productivity, improved public health and greater innovation. Enhanced individuals could contribute to solving complex global challenges, such as climate change, disease and poverty by leveraging their augmented capabilities.

As with any new tool, technology or advancement, it can and likely will lead to both progressive improvements to the human condition while also posing these possible risks.

This aspect of The Singularity also raises important ethical and regulatory questions. Policymakers and ethicists must address issues related to the safety, accessibility and fairness of enabling technologies that boost biological processes. Nick Bostrom argues, "The responsible development and regulation of enhancement technologies are essential to ensure their benefits are widely shared and their risks are mitigated" (Bostrom, 2014). Ensuring that these technologies are developed and deployed in an equitable and responsible manner is crucial for maximizing their benefits and minimizing potential harms.

Sociologist Sherry Turkle notes, "The merging of humans and technology will require us to rethink our social norms and cultural values, as we navigate the new landscape of human-technology interaction" (Turkle, 2011). Clearly the integration of advanced technologies into society may lead to changes in social norms and cultural values. As individuals adopt new forms of enhancement and augmentation, traditional notions of human abilities and limitations may be challenged and there is no doubt that this will lead to a reevaluation of societal expectations and the development of new cultural practices that embrace technological integration.

Impacts on Geopolitics

The geopolitical implications of human/technology assimilation are equally significant as nations, ideology-bound treaty or trade partners and global powers compete for technological dominance and strategic advantages. Enhanced cognitive and physical capabilities could provide competitive edges in areas such as economic productivity, military strength and scientific innovation. Nations that lead in the development and deployment of human enhancement technologies may gain significant geopolitical influence, shaping global norms and policies. As political scientist James Hughes notes, "The race for technological dominance in human enhancement could reshape global power dynamics, with profound implications for international relations and security" (Hughes, 2004). This could lead to new forms of international competition and cooperation as countries seek to harness the potential of these technologies while addressing shared ethical and security concerns.

The potential for these same human enhancement technologies to be used in military applications is particularly concerning. Enhanced soldiers with superior physical and cognitive abilities would revolutionize warfare leading to new forms of conflict and escalation and this underscores the importance of considering the ethical implications of using enhancement technologies for military purposes, which must be carefully considered to prevent potential abuses and ensure compliance with international humanitarian norms. As military ethicist Patrick Lin argues, "The use of enhancement technologies in the military raises serious ethical and legal questions that must be addressed to ensure their responsible use" (Lin, 2013). This idea has been explored in numerous pop culture formats including film, graphic novels, fiction and video games and the outcomes are rarely presented as optimistic visions of the future.

Additionally, the development and deployment of human enhancement technologies could lead to shifts in global economic power. Countries that invest heavily in research and development in this area may experience significant economic growth and innovation, gaining a competitive advantage in the global market. This could lead to changes in trade dynamics, labor markets and international economic policies. As economist Robert Atkinson notes, "The economic impact of human enhancement technologies could be transformative, driving growth and innovation in ways that reshape the global economy" (Atkinson, 2019).

Philosophical Implications: What Does It Mean to Be Human?

The Singularity brings up analyses and debate about what it means to be human and the core of human existence. As people enhance their bodies and minds with technology it becomes increasingly complex to grasp the essence of humanity.

A crucial philosophical query in this realm tackles the subjects of consciousness and self-awareness. If advanced technologies allow us to boost or even replicate human thought processes, how does this impact our understanding of consciousness? Philosopher Thomas Metzinger tackles this in his book *The Ego Tunnel; The Science of the Mind and the Myth of the Self* where he explores how our sense of self is a construct generated by the brain. Metzinger suggests that our self-perception may be an illusion and advancements in neuroscience and technology could reshape this perception. He emphasizes that as we incorporate technology into our own physical functions, we need to rethink how we perceive ourselves and our connection to our physical bodies (Metzinger, 2009).

The integration of humans and technology also challenges ideas about identity and independence. As people incorporate technologies into their bodies and minds their sense of self could become intertwined with devices and systems. This situation raises questions about autonomy and the level of control individuals can maintain over their enhanced selves. Ethicist Julian Savulescu astutely pointed out that "enhancement technologies may blur the distinction between human and machine challenging our notions of autonomy and self-integrity" (Savulescu, 2011).

This scenario also prompts inquiries into how it affects our understanding of mortality and the essence of life. If individuals can improve their functions and potentially achieve immortality through methods like uploading of their neural imprint, what implications does this hold for our perception of life and death? Transhumanist philosopher Max More argues that the pursuit of life extension and enhancement technologies is a continuation of humanity's pursuit for self-betterment and transcendence. He suggests, "The convergence of humans with technology presents opportunities for life extension and a reimagining of what it means to exist" (More, 2013).

Ethicist John Harris similarly highlights that advancements in abilities through technology could change how we think about ethics, potentially leading to new ways of ethical reasoning and behavior (Harris, 2007). As people gain the power to boost their emotional skills, they might adopt novel approaches to moral thinking and ethical conduct. This shift could prompt a reassessment of established frameworks and the emergence of moral principles that embrace technological enhancements.

The combination of technology into life also introduces uncertainty regarding the essence of creativity and artistic expression. Artist and futurist Natasha Vita-More proposes that fusing humans with technology will unlock avenues for expression and cultural innovation ushering in a new phase of creativity and exploration (Vita More, 2015). As individuals enhance their creative capacities it is conceivable that they may create forms of artistic and cultural expression that go beyond traditional boundaries. This scenario could spark a renaissance in creativity fueled by the abilities of technologically enhanced individuals.

Exploring the fusion of humanity and technology poses questions about our essence, touching on many of these topics such as self-awareness, individuality, freedom, lifespan, moral principles and innovation. As we venture into this territory of blending life with technology it becomes crucial to weigh the advantages and drawbacks mindfully. We need to guarantee that these advancements are handled with care and used in a way that honors values while safeguarding the welfare of everyone involved.

Wrapping Up The Singularity

If you think this was enjoyable to get your head around, just wait!

Exploring The Singularity unveils an often perplexing and uncertain outlook for the future where artificial intelligence, biotechnology, nanotechnology and other cutting-edge technologies will fundamentally reshape human existence.

In this section we've explored the elements of The Singularity touching upon the progress shaping our future, the philosophical dilemmas it presents and how it could impact human evolution. AI, with its deep learning capabilities and emulated neural networks is set to enhance our functions and change how we engage with the world. Biotechnology and genetic engineering offer chances to improve abilities and combat diseases. Nanotechnology and BCI's open possibilities for enhancing humans in ways that seamlessly integrate with our systems. However, these advancements also bring about numerous societal quandaries. Issues such as inequality, privacy risks and redefining identity require careful thought and proactive regulation. As we approach this era, it is crucial to address these concerns to ensure that everyone can access The Singularity's benefits equitably.

As we move on to the next part of this paper, we will shift our attention to The Simulation Hypothesis. While The Singularity and The Simulation Hypothesis may seem unrelated at first glance, a closer look reveals connections between these two theories. Exploring The Simulation Hypothesis allows us to dive into concepts of quantum physics, information and the multiverse, setting the stage for understanding how these ideas transect with the advancements driving The Singularity. In the following sections we will discuss how merging The Singularity with The Simulation Hypothesis offers a framework for comprehending the universe, consciousness and human existence. Pretty heady stuff, right? This combination not only questions our long-standing beliefs but also presents thought-provoking insights into the nature of reality and our role within it.

The Simulation Hypothesis

In Rizwan Virk's book, *The Simulation Hypothesis* the author proposes that our world is actually a simulation crafted by an advanced society. According to Virk, as our capabilities in computer science, virtual reality and artificial intelligence progress, the idea of constructing a reality identical to our own becomes more plausible. His theory is based on the concept that if creating sophisticated simulations is achievable and if civilizations across the universe possess this capability, it is more probable than not that we are currently existing within one of these simulations.

Virk's hypothesis provides a framework for interpreting anomalies and inexplicable occurrences within our perceived reality. These anomalies may involve situations where the laws of physics appear to be altered or events that defy reasoning. By exploring the notion that these anomalies could be glitches or intentional features of a simulation setting, Virk's theory offers a perspective on reality, consciousness and the essence of existence itself. It suggests that what we perceive as 'real' might closely resemble a video game or virtual realm. According to Virk "in case we exist within a simulation the oddities and enigmas present in our surroundings could be elements meant to provoke us to ponder the essence of our existence" (Virk, 2019).

I did mention in the Introduction that it may seem a bit 'out there' at first. However, consider one fascinating theory from modern physics: the Holographic Principle. Originating from research in black hole thermodynamics and string theory, this principle proposes that all information within a space volume can be represented by data on its boundary. Essentially our three-dimensional reality could be a projection from a two-dimensional surface similar to how holograms operate. Physicist Leonard Susskind, an advocate for the principle elaborates that "although we don't perceive our world as a hologram at its core level reality is two dimensional and our three-dimensional world emerges as an illusion from it" (Susskind, 2008). This concept strengthens the idea that our perceived reality could actually be artificially created in accordance with The Simulation Hypothesis.

Before we get into specifics on the startlingly convincing work that encompasses Virk's theory, it helps to take a peek into the core concepts of quantum mechanics, the field of physics that explains how particles behave at subatomic levels. Quantum mechanics, despite being relatively young and spanning only a century of study, has transformed our comprehension of the cosmos. So, its implications are profound and expansive.

In 1900, Max Planck introduced quantization suggesting that energy is released in units known as quanta. This departure from physics continuous energy distribution was revolutionary. Albert Einstein expanded on this notion in 1905 when he proposed that light comprises quanta called photons carrying energy proportionate to their frequency. This marked a milestone in quantum theory's evolution. In 1924, Louis de Broglie proposed that particles, like electrons, demonstrate wave particle-like characteristics; a concept referred to as wave particle duality proven through an experiment called the Davisson Germer experiment in 1927. The results of the Davisson-Germer experiment concretely established the validity of quantum mechanics and advanced our scientific understanding of the subatomic world. And Erwin Schrödinger and Werner Heisenberg each further independently formulated the principles of quantum mechanics in the mid-1920s. Schrödinger's wave equation explains how a system's quantum state evolves over time while Heisenberg's matrix mechanics offers an equivalent framework.

Key Principles of Quantum Mechanics

In quantum mechanics, a system can exist in multiple states at once until observed. This concept is captured by Schrödinger's wave function which outlines the likelihood of finding a particle at a particular position. This concept is referred to as superposition. Take, for example a quantum particle, like an electron, which can exist in different positions or energy states all at once. It is not restricted to two conditions; it can encompass a mix of states based on the system and circumstances.

Quantum entanglement and nonlocality present some of the most perplexing phenomena in quantum mechanics. Albert Einstein famously referred to entanglement as "spooky action at a distance," expressing his discomfort with the idea that particles could influence each other instantaneously across vast distances. Despite Einstein's reservations, numerous experiments have confirmed the reality of quantum entanglement and nonlocality. Most notably, Bell's Theorem proposed by physicist John Bell in 1964, showed that no local hidden variable theory could reproduce the predictions of quantum mechanics. Experiments conducted by Alain Aspect and others in the 1980's provided empirical evidence supporting quantum entanglement and ruled out local hidden variable theories. Entanglement occurs when particles become interconnected so that their quantum states are linked regardless of distance. When one entangled particle is measured it instantaneously influences the state of its counterpart. This introduces the idea of nonlocality which describes how particles connected in the past remain linked allowing one particle's state to instantly impact another regardless of their distance. The concept is famously illustrated by the Einstein Podolsky Rosen (EPR) paradox and further confirmed through Bell's subsequent experiments. Nonlocality suggests that information can be exchanged between particles faster than light speed revealing a profound interconnectedness within the quantum realm.

To make quantum mechanics more understandable, let's consider some analogies and examples (trust me, it took a while before I got it and you may want to take special note of one key book in the references at the end of this essay. It's called - *Quantum Physics for Beginners who Flunked Math and Science: Quantum Mechanics and Physics Made Easy Guide in Plain Simple English*. For those of us who aren't natural STEM students, it's a must!)

Okay, so here we go - think of light behaving both as a wave and a particle. Picture a wave passing through two slits in a barrier and forming an interference pattern on a screen behind it. Surprisingly, even when individual photons are sent through the slits one-by-one they still contribute to this interference pattern showcasing wave characteristics despite being particles. Consider Superposition as tossing a coin and catching it before seeing which side it landed on. Until observed the coin is both heads and tails simultaneously. Similarly in quantum mechanics particles exist in undefined states simultaneously until observed.

When it comes to Entanglement, it helps to picture having two entangled dice. When you roll one die and it displays a six, the other die, *no matter where it is*, will always also show a six. This connection over all distances is a key feature of quantum entanglement.

So, you see, even if you did struggle with mathematics in high school, it can still all make some sense to us. Don't worry either way, even quantum physicists often refer to the fact that some of what they study is hard to comprehend, even for them.

There have been crucial advancements in science and technology thanks to quantum mechanics – some might even call them quantum leaps (that's a cheesy pun – apologies). Quantum computing, for example uses superposition and entanglement principles to carry out computations at speeds and capacities that blow away the processing abilities of traditional computers. As previously mentioned, Google made headlines in 2019 when it announced that its quantum computer, Sycamore had achieved quantum supremacy by completing a task that would be impossible for normal computers (Arute et al., 2019). This accomplishment marked an advancement in the field of quantum computing and showcased the potential of this technology to transform various sectors such as cryptography, materials science and artificial intelligence.

The field of quantum mechanics also raises thought-provoking questions about The Simulation Hypothesis. The unique behaviors exhibited by quantum systems, like superposition and entanglement can be viewed as characteristics of a simulated reality. If our universe is indeed a simulation, these quantum phenomena may be attributed to underlying processes. For example, the observer effect where observing a system collapses its wave function into a specific state can be likened to rendering mechanisms in video games where the environment comes into view only when interacted with by the player. This concept is aligned with the idea of a simulation that efficiently manages resources by displaying details only when needed. Additionally, the pixelated characteristics of the universe indicated by energy levels and the quantization of quantities suggest a hidden grid or lattice structure which very much could serve as the structure of the environment in the same way as pixels function on a computer screen.

Quantum Mechanics and the Nature of Reality: The Observer Effect

One of the most intriguing aspects of quantum mechanics is the observer effect, where the act of measurement influences the state of a quantum system – and one that also plays into elements of The Simulation Hypothesis. In classical physics, measurements can be made without affecting the system being observed. However, in quantum mechanics the act of measuring a particle's position collapses its wave function forcing it into a definite state. This phenomenon suggests that reality is not fixed until it is observed, challenging our traditional understanding of an objective, independent reality.

The observer effect has profound implications for The Simulation Hypothesis. Rizwan Virk argues, "If our universe is a simulation, the observer effect could be interpreted as a rendering process similar to how video games generate graphics only when needed" (Virk, 2019). This efficiency saves computational resources by only rendering details when they are observed, not at all dissimilar to how a quantum system collapses into a definite state upon measurement.

Quantum Superposition and Many-Worlds Interpretation

Quantum superposition, where a particle exists in multiple states simultaneously, is another fundamental principle of quantum mechanics that we covered above. The famous thought experiment known as Schrödinger's cat illustrates this concept. In this experiment, a cat is placed in a sealed box with a radioactive atom, a Geiger counter and a vial of poison. If the Geiger counter detects radiation, the poison is released, killing the cat. If not, the cat remains alive. According to quantum mechanics, the cat is simultaneously alive and dead until the box is opened and the state is observed. A related interpretation of quantum superposition is the Many-Worlds Interpretation, proposed by Hugh Everett III in 1957. This interpretation suggests that all possible outcomes of a quantum event actually occur in separate, branching universes. In the context of Schrödinger's cat, there would be one universe where the cat is alive and another where the cat is dead. These branching universes form a multiverse of parallel realities.

The Many-Worlds Interpretation has intriguing implications for The Simulation Hypothesis. Virk states, "If our universe is a simulation, the branching of parallel universes could be a computational process where all possible outcomes are calculated and exist in separate simulations" (Virk, 2019). This perspective aligns with the idea of a multiverse, where each universe represents a different simulation with varying parameters and outcomes. We will cover this in more detail in a section dedicated to the Multiverse.

Quantum Field Theory

Quantum field theory (QFT) is a theoretical framework that combines classical field theory, special relativity and quantum mechanics. QFT treats particles as excitations in underlying fields with each type of particle corresponding to a different field. QFT has been remarkably successful in describing fundamental interactions and particles. The development of the Standard Model of particle physics, which describes the electromagnetic, weak and strong nuclear forces, is based on QFT and the discovery of the Higgs Boson in 2012 at the Large Hadron Collider provided further validation of the Standard Model. The predictive power of QFT suggests that the universe operates according to deeply embedded principles of symmetry and invariance. In the context of The Simulation Hypothesis, these principles could be the underlying rules of the simulated environment, encoded into the computational framework governing the simulation.

The Role of Consciousness in Quantum Mechanics

One of the most controversial and debated aspects of quantum mechanics is the role of consciousness in the measurement process. As a side note, this is what actually got me looking at quantum physics in the first place. My father, a history professor, taught a course on consciousness prior to retiring that seemed to spark his interest more than many pure history subjects. Eventually, after years of hearing about this beguiling world of consciousness studies, I had to check it out. That started me down a process over several years where my non-fiction reading was fixated on consciousness. I've since come to appreciate that if you study consciousness at any level, eventually, whether you want to or not, you are going to find yourself exiting onto an off-ramp that heads directly towards the neighborhood of quantum mechanics. And then, since I had already found myself engrossed in The Singularity idea, it all started connecting with technology and AI.

Some interpretations of quantum mechanics suggest that the observer's consciousness is necessary to collapse the wave function and bring about a definitive outcome. This idea, known as the 'consciousness causes collapse' hypothesis has been explored by several physicists and philosophers. Physicist Eugene Wigner proposed that consciousness plays a fundamental role in the measurement process, suggesting that the wave function collapse occurs only when observed by a conscious being. Similarly, John von Neumann's interpretation of quantum mechanics claims that the conscious mind is necessary for the collapse of the wave function.

These interpretations have led to speculative theories about the connection between consciousness and the nature of reality. If consciousness is indeed fundamental to the measurement process, it could imply that our conscious minds are integral to the functioning of the simulated environment. In other words, our awareness might be a crucial component of the computational processes underlying our observed reality.

At the intersection of human awareness and quantum mechanics lies a fascinating and peculiar crossroad that is constantly evolving. Recent advancements in this field highlight the profound implications of merging human consciousness with the mysterious principles of quantum mechanics. George Musser's enlightening work, *Incorporating Ourselves into the Equation: How Physicists are Investigating Human Consciousness and AI to Unravel the Universe's Mysteries*, expands horizons and stimulates philosophical thought on this significant intersection. It is so absorbing and interrelated with The Simulation Hypothesis, we just have to delve into it more.

Musser's Journey into Quantum Consciousness

Musser's exploration into the realm where physics meets human consciousness provides a captivating narrative that challenges conventional understandings of reality. Like Virk and Kurzweil's work, his is a close second as a foundational theory supporting The Simularity Proposition. He proposes that to unravel the universe's greatest mysteries we must examine the observer – ourselves. This idea aligns with philosophical inquiries into the nature of existence and perception. If quantum mechanics suggests that observing can change or can essentially define a particle's state, what can we deduce about consciousness's role in shaping our reality? "Consciousness is not just a byproduct of biological processes but an integral part of the fabric of reality," Musser argues, suggesting that our very act of observation could be influencing the universe in ways we have yet to fully understand (Musser, 2021). His perspective calls for a reevaluation of the Cartesian separation of mind and body, promoting a more comprehensive understanding of consciousness as a fundamental aspect of the universe.

The implications of this quantum view of consciousness are significant and far-reaching. It challenges the traditional mechanistic view of the universe, which sees reality as a collection of independent, interacting parts and instead promotes a more holistic, interconnected understanding of existence. "If the observer effect in quantum mechanics shows us anything, it's that the act of observation is a powerful force," Musser notes, highlighting the potential for consciousness to play a crucial role in the very fabric of reality (Musser, 2021). This perspective encourages us to view consciousness not as an emergent property of complex neural interactions but as an intrinsic aspect of the universe. Such a view not only transforms our understanding of the mind but also suggests that consciousness and reality are deeply intertwined in ways that challenge existing paradigms.

As we speed towards the AI revolution, Musser's insights into studying consciousness through quantum mechanics become even more relevant. The pursuit of giving machines a semblance of human-like consciousness raises crucial ethical and philosophical questions. If consciousness can be viewed as a quantum process, the creation of AI systems capable of mimicking or even surpassing human cognitive processes opens a world of mystifying possibilities and dilemmas. Musser highlights the ethical dimensions of this pursuit, questioning the implications of creating conscious machines. "If AI were to achieve a form of consciousness, what rights and responsibilities would we have towards these entities?" he asks, pushing us to consider more moral implications of our technological advancements (Musser, 2021). The intersection of AI and quantum consciousness not only offers the potential for groundbreaking technological developments but also necessitates a profound ethical and philosophical reevaluation.

Within the context of Musser's perspective, recent advancements in quantum computing and neuroscience further support this intersection of quantum mechanics and consciousness. Researchers have made significant strides in understanding the brain's quantum processes, suggesting that elements of human cognition may indeed operate at the quantum level (Hameroff and Penrose, 2014). The leap in computational power we discussed with regards to quantum computing also opens new avenues for simulating neural processes and understanding consciousness. As these fields converge, the possibility of creating AI with quantum-enhanced cognitive capabilities becomes more plausible. Such advancements could lead to machines that not only perform tasks but also exhibit a form of consciousness capable of introspection and complex decision-making.

While quantum mind theories remain speculative and controversial, they offer intriguing possibilities for understanding the relationship between consciousness and quantum mechanics. If consciousness arises from quantum processes, it might be intimately connected to the underlying computational framework of the simulated reality. This perspective aligns with Virk's proposition of The Simulation Hypothesis intimating that our conscious experiences are part of the simulation's complex information processing. Virk's exploration into The Simulation Hypothesis suggests that these quantum phenomena could stem from underlying processes where phenomenon like quantum entanglement and superposition might be clarified by a concealed layer enabling information exchange: "Quantum entanglement could be seen as evidence of an underlying computational framework that allows for instantaneous information transfer" (Virk, 2019).

When we look into The Simulation Hypothesis further it's important to think about how it could change our views on reality, consciousness and existence. The connection between quantum mechanics and The Simulation Hypothesis provides a way to reconsider our role in the universe and the rules that shape our lives.

About Simulations

Understanding the role of technology in simulation is helpful in further consideration of The Simulation Hypothesis and it requires tracing the historical evolution of computational technologies from early mechanical devices to modern digital computers and sophisticated simulation technologies.

The concept of mechanical computation dates to ancient times, with devices like the abacus and the Antikythera mechanism, an ancient Greek analog computer used to predict astronomical positions and eclipses. However, the foundation for modern computational technology was laid in the 19th century with Charles Babbage's designs for the Analytical Engine, a mechanical general-purpose computer. Though never completed in his lifetime, Babbage's work laid the groundwork for the digital computers that would emerge in the 20th century (Swade, 2000).

The digital revolution began in earnest with the development of the first electronic digital computers during World War II. Machines like the ENIAC (Electronic Numerical Integrator and Computer) and the Colossus were capable of performing complex calculations at unprecedented speeds. These early computers were used primarily for military applications such as code-breaking and ballistic trajectory calculations (Rojas & Hashagen, 2000). And then, the post-war era saw rapid advancements in computing technology, driven by innovations such as the transistor invented by John Bardeen, Walter Brattain and William Shockley in 1947, and the integrated circuit developed by Jack Kilby and Robert Noyce in the late 1950s. These innovations led to the miniaturization and increased power of computers making them more accessible for a variety of applications.

As computing power grew so did the ability to create real simulations (an oxymoronic term, I know, 'real simulations' – but really, they are real).

Early digital simulations were used in scientific research to model physical systems, such as weather patterns and nuclear reactions. Later, the development of graphical user interfaces (GUIs) and advances in computer graphics during the 1960's and 1970's further enhanced simulation capabilities and the creation of computer-generated imagery (CGI) allowed for the visualization of complex data and the simulation of realistic environments. These advancements paved the way for modern video games and virtual reality technologies, which now can create immersive simulated experiences.

Today, the role of technology in simulation has expanded significantly, driven by advancements in AI, quantum computing and VR. These technologies are not only enhancing our ability to create detailed and realistic simulations but are also providing new insights into the nature of reality itself. Artificial intelligence, particularly machine learning, has revolutionized the field of simulation where now machine learning algorithms can analyze vast amounts of data, identify patterns and make predictions which are essential capabilities and preconditions for creating realistic simulations. For example, AI-driven simulations are used in fields such as climate science to model and predict weather patterns with increasing accuracy (Schmidt et al., 2017).

AI is also used in the development of autonomous systems and robotics where simulations are employed to train and test algorithms in virtual environments before deploying them in the real world. This approach reduces risks and costs associated with real-world testing. And AI-driven simulations are increasingly used in the entertainment industry, particularly in video games and virtual reality. Game developers use AI to create intelligent non-player characters (NPC's) that can adapt to the player's actions, creating more dynamic and engaging lifelike experiences.

Now let's jump back into the world of quantum computing for a moment since one of the most promising applications of quantum computing is in the field of – you guessed it - simulation. Quantum computers can simulate systems more efficiently than classical computers, which is essential for understanding complex physical phenomena and this capability has profound implications (Feynman, 1982). In the context of The Simulation Hypothesis, quantum computing could provide the computational power necessary to run large-scale simulations of entire universes. The ability to perform parallel computations and handle vast amounts of data suggests that quantum computers could simulate the behavior of all particles in a universe, providing a plausible mechanism for the realization of a simulated reality.

And it's practically here now! I experience it every weekend when my daughter and I have the pleasure of playing the incredible open-word video game *Elden Ring* in a simulated, virtual online environment through our PlayStations. VR and AR technologies have transformed our ability to create and interact within simulated environments. VR immerses users in fully digital environments, while AR overlays digital information onto the real world. Both technologies rely on sophisticated hardware and software to create realistic and responsive experiences. Within The Simulation Hypothesis, VR and AR offer a glimpse into the potential of creating convincing simulated realities. Current VR systems, such as the Oculus Rift and HTC Vive use high-resolution displays, motion tracking and haptic feedback to create immersive experiences. As these technologies continue to advance, they could eventually become indistinguishable from reality, supporting the notion that our perceived reality might be a simulation. If you've played *Grand Turismo* on a VR headset, mounted a winged banshee on the Pandora 3D *Avatar Flight of Passage* at Disney World in Orlando, Florida or were fortunate enough to experience the future of entertainment by taking in a *U2* concert at the *Sphere* in Las Vegas, you have to have a sense of just how 'real' simulations are becoming and, more critically, have some thoughts on how realistic they will become in, say, a decade from now.

In addition, the development of BCI's, which we covered in our overview of The Singularity, hold the promise of even deeper integration between humans and simulated environments. BCI's allow for direct communication between the brain and external devices and enabling users to control virtual environments with their thoughts. This technology has the potential to create seamless and intuitive interactions with simulated realities, further distorting the line between the real and the virtual.

Looking ahead, several emerging technologies could further enhance our ability to create and maintain large-scale simulations. These technologies include advanced AI, next-generation quantum computers and novel computing paradigms such as neuromorphic computing. The development of advanced AI capable of performing tasks with human-like intelligence will significantly enhance the creation of simulations. AI systems that can understand and replicate human behavior, emotions and decision-making processes will be essential for creating realistic and dynamic simulated environments. And one related and promising avenue of research is the development of artificial general intelligence (AGI) which aims to create AI systems with the ability to perform any intellectual task that a human can do. AGI would enable the creation of NPC's and virtual entities that can think, learn, interact and adapt autonomously making simulated environments more lifelike and interactive. Researchers are currently working on developing more stable and scalable quantum computers, with the goal of achieving fault-tolerant quantum computing. One area of focus is the development of quantum error correction techniques, which are essential for maintaining the integrity of quantum computations. Advances in this field could lead to quantum computers capable of performing protracted and complex simulations without errors, making large-scale simulations more feasible.

Neuromorphic computing is an emerging field that seeks to mimic the structure and function of the human brain in computer hardware. Neuromorphic systems use artificial neurons and synapses to process information in a manner similar to the brain, enabling more efficient and parallel processing of data. Neuromorphic computing has the potential to revolutionize the field of simulation by providing new ways to model and simulate complex systems. For example, neuromorphic chips could be used to simulate neural networks and brain activity with unprecedented detail and accuracy and this capability could be particularly valuable for simulating human behavior and cognition in virtual environments.

Although The Simulation Hypothesis has developed more extensively in recent years due the innovations as well as our expanding knowledgebase through technological expansion, the idea that our reality might be an illusion is not new. Philosophers throughout history have pondered the nature of reality and the possibility that our perceptions might not correspond to an objective external world.

The Chinese philosopher Zhuangzi raised thought provoking questions about reality through his known dream involving a butterfly. In this dream he found it challenging to discern whether he was a man dreaming of being a butterfly or a butterfly dreaming of being a man (Zhuangzi 369 286 BCE).

It is tempting to summarize Plato's Allegory of the Cave in this section; however, I have forced myself to suppress the temptation to get into it as an historical example that questions our perception of reality. It is an overused and obvious reference (it was covered in the first-year undergrad philosophy course I took decades ago) and I have already indulged in one of these overdone examples with Schrödinger's cat! So, we'll go almost as conventional and talk about René Descartes instead and his notion that our perceptions could be influenced by a demon prompting us to doubt the reliability of our senses and the existence of an external world. Descartes hypothetical scenario paved the way for skepticism and philosophical investigations into reality (Descartes, 1641). Then later, in the 20th century philosopher Hilary Putnam introduced the 'brain in a vat' thought experiment. This scenario involves keeping a brain in a vat and supplying it with inputs through advanced computing systems to create an illusion of an external world. Putnam utilized this concept to probe the boundaries of our knowledge and contemplate whether our experiences could be artificially constructed (Putnam, 1981). For any of us who have watched the original movie *The Matrix* - the brain in a vat concept is poignant.

While these philosophical reflections offer intriguing perspectives on reality, in more recent decades The Simulation Hypothesis has emerged as a plausible existential consideration due mostly to exponential technological progress. The rapid increase in computational power fueled by Moore's Law, along with the emergence of quantum computing has laid the groundwork for a new layer of support when it comes to the concept of large-scale simulations. What's most fascinating is how recent technological progress has propelled The Simulation Hypothesis into a realm that demands scrutiny while also adding weight to the importance of understanding and preparing for The Singularity. The Simulation Hypothesis has transitioned from speculative cogitation to a scientifically plausible concept owing to these technological breakthroughs. Rizwan Virk notes, "The rapid increase in computing power and the development of artificial intelligence and quantum computing have enabled us to bridge the gap between philosophical ideas and the potential reality of a simulated world" (Virk, 2019).

The following paragraph represents the most 'eye-opening' facet of The Simulation Hypothesis. When I first began probing these theories, I remember reading Virk's perspective regarding the idea that modern science has demonstrated how even the smallest of particles in our universe are reducible to pieces of information. This was my 'wait, what!?' moment. Quantum physics has brought about shifts in how we comprehend the universe and scientists have uncovered that at its core the universe seems to be made up more from information than substance. This concept suggests that our perception of reality could be akin to a simulation. As we've discussed, the principles of quantum mechanics indicate that particles exist in a state of uncertainty until they are directly observed implying that observation itself influences the fabric of the universe. Virk goes deep into this concept in his work, drawing parallels between quantum phenomena and the dynamics seen in simulated worlds. He explains how similar elements in a video game are generated only when a player focuses on them and draws the parallel to how particles in our universe remain probabilistic until observed. These advancements in science bring sharp credibility to The Simulation Hypothesis offering insights that were previously beyond reach.

The notion that our universe functions based on principles that are very alike to those observed in computer simulations awakens people to the idea that our physical reality could potentially be a creation. This shift in perspective is backed by the understanding that various occurrences at the quantum level align with the operations of simulations where information and computation play quintessential roles. Viewing the universe as a simulation offers an interpretation for some of quantum physics most baffling aspects, such as entanglement and superposition. These puzzling phenomena which have confounded scientists for years become more comprehensible when examined through an information-theory lens. Within a simulated reality the instantaneous connection between particles (or, more accurately, particles in numerous potential states) to observation can be perceived as preprogrammed functions within an extensive computational structure. As we continue to grasp more of quantum mechanics and information theory, The Simulation Hypothesis gains increasing acceptance. The concept of inhabiting an existence once confined to science fiction realms is now receiving attention from physicists, philosophers and technologists alike. This hypothesis not only challenges our understanding of reality but it also prompts us to think about the profound implications of living in a universe fundamentally constructed of information.

If that isn't thought-provoking enough, let's take some time to contemplate the multiverse next!

Multiverse Theory

The idea of the multiverse has become a theme in entertainment that has been captivating audiences around the globe for years. A prime example is the movie and novel *Ready Player One* which depicts a future where virtual reality technology has evolved to create a world known as the OASIS. Within this realm individuals can escape reality and venture into worlds with unique characteristics and possibilities. While a work of fiction, this narrative mirrors aspects of the multiverse concept and acts as a pathway to explore the implications of The Simulation Hypothesis.

The theory of the multiverse suggests that our universe is one among many realities that exist simultaneously. These universes, collectively referred to as the multiverse, could differ in their laws, constants and initial setups. The notion of multiple and parallel universes has been examined in scientific and philosophical discussions shedding more light on how we perceive reality and consider theories like The Simulation Hypothesis.

A prominent scientific basis for the multiverse theory stems from quantum mechanics through theories that Virk expounds in his writing on the subject. Physicist Hugh Everett put forth the Many-Worlds Interpretation (MWI) in 1957 which suggests that every possible outcome of a quantum event happens in its universe. In this view, whenever or not an observation and a successive quantum measurement is taken, the universe splits into branches each of which moves forward with absolute individual results that proceed with their own variables and consequences in concurrent fashion. This concept of diverging universes aligns with The Simulation Hypothesis.

Cosmological theories additionally lend credence to the notion of a multiverse. One such theory is inflation, first proposed by physicist Alan Guth in the 1980's. According to this concept our universe exists as one bubble within a multiverse that continues to grow infinitely. Quantum fluctuations caused specific regions to cease inflating and form distinct universes while others kept expanding resulting in an infinite number of bubble universes. These bubble universes may possess varying properties and constants rendering each one distinct from the others.

According to string theory there exists a 'landscape' of universes, each corresponding to different solutions of the theory's equations. This landscape multiverse encompasses a number of distinct universes, each possessing its distinct set of physical laws and constants (Susskind, 2008). The landscape multiverse proposes that our universe is one among an infinite number of potential configurations. If The Simulation Hypothesis is valid, it is possible that advanced entities could simulate universes within this landscape, delivering a multitude of physical realities with the implications of altering fundamental constants.

Virk further examines the concept that our existence might be one of numerous simulated universes, each potentially controlled by distinct parameters and histories. A key focus of Virk's research is the notion that advanced civilizations, having surpassed our technological prowess, could create and oversee multiple simulations. This concept expands on The Simulation Hypothesis by proposing not only the possibility of us living in a simulation but also suggesting the existence of variations of simulated realities each with its own distinct timeline, foundational rule set and rendered events. According to Virk "if we have the ability to craft simulations of reality then an advanced society could generate simulations with diverse historical outcomes" (Virk, 2021). Leveraging principles from quantum mechanics to bolster his premise regarding these multidimensional universes, Virk references physicist John Wheeler's delayed choice experiment. This experiment implies that future measurements can influence the result of an event thereby challenging notions of time and causality. It suggests that various outcomes remain possible until a measurement is taken, not unlike the observer effect, and one that supports how multiple universes could be invoked through the process of observation itself: "The delayed choice experiment hints at the presence of realities merging into one observed reality upon measurement " elaborates Virk (Virk, 2021).

Virk's multiverse theory explores the connections it shares with *déjà vu* and the Mandela Effect. These occurrences, where reconstructed memories differ from the individual's accepted reality, could potentially stem from the mixing or blending of simulated timelines. Virk implies that such instances could represent glitches in the simulation or indications of interactions occurring within experiences that exist among variegated simulations. He suggests that experiencing *déjà vu* and encountering the

Mandela Effect may offer insights into the simulated paths our reality might follow (Virk, 2021).

In another of his works, *The Simulated Multiverse*, Virk also inquiries into how the concept of a multiverse can serve as a construct for comprehending and harmonizing interpretations of quantum mechanics. Within this multiverse framework, both the Copenhagen interpretation, suggesting particles exist in a state of superposition until observed and the Many-Worlds Interpretation, proposing that each quantum event gives rise to new potential universe, can coexist. According to Virk, by envisioning the universe as a sequence of simulations we can accommodate both wave function collapse and the proliferation of realities (Virk, 2021). This is where quantum physics and the possibility of our existence being represented through multiple simulated realities come together to form a compelling perspective.

Another thought-inspiring aspect of The Simulation Hypothesis revolves around the conceptions of how multiverse theory ultimately impacts our perception of time. Virk proposes that time, as an element within a given universe, may not follow a definitive path but rather unfold as a series of distinct events that can be altered by adjusting the simulation's settings. This concept relates to the notion of 'time loops' or 'resets' within a simulation, enabling the repetition of scenarios with outcomes. He points out that in a multiverse time could resemble a medium rather than a continuous stream (Virk, 2021).

Returning for a moment to the idea that all piece parts of our reality are reducible to information, this is where the multiverse again intersects with our understanding of physics which regards the universe, at its core, as information. From this perspective, our perception of reality stems from informational processes. Virk concludes that if our universe is founded on information then multiple simulated realities could exist as configurations of the underlying data (Virk, 2021).

Looking ahead at The Singularity event, discussed extensively in the first part of this essay, where various technologies converge and ultimately assimilated with our biology, we see a foundation being laid for The Simulation Hypothesis. As we approach this point in time, advancements in AI and quantum computing will empower us to create simulations that can potentially encompass worlds with unique characteristics and their own laws of physics. The rapid expansion of knowledge and computing capabilities enables us to bridge the gap between imaginative musings and scientific possibilities. As we push the boundaries of technology and understanding, The Simulation Hypothesis emerges as an explanation for the core fabric of our reality.

One of the most common criticisms of The Simulation Hypothesis is the lack of direct evidence. Critics argue that while there are intriguing hints and indirect evidence there is no definitive proof that we are living in a simulation. However, proponents of the hypothesis argue that the very nature of a simulation would make direct evidence difficult or, in fact, impossible to obtain. If the simulation is designed to be indistinguishable from reality, then the lack of direct evidence is precisely what we would expect to find (Bostrom, 2003). If we think about it more fully, however, the fact is that despite even our most recent advancements in science, we still have only a minimal understanding of our universe. In many respects, we are still like the ancient Greeks staring up at the stars thousands of years ago. The ancient Greeks believed the stars to be divine and eternal objects, often associating them with gods and myths. They thought the stars were fixed on a celestial sphere that revolved around the Earth which they considered the center of the universe. Prominent Greek philosophers like Pythagoras and Aristotle contributed to these ideas, which prevailed from around the 6th century BCE to the Hellenistic period. Since that time our understanding and theories have progressed, however, the universe in all its incomprehensible vastness remains, for the most part, a giant mystery.

Another criticism is that the computational power required to simulate an entire universe is beyond the capabilities of any conceivable technology. This criticism assumes that the simulation must be run at the same level of detail as our observed universe. In reality (no pun intended) the simulation could employ various optimization techniques, such as focusing computational resources on areas of interest and using simplified models for less critical regions. Additionally, advancements in quantum computing could provide the necessary computational power to run large-scale simulations (Lloyd, 2006).

Some critics argue that The Simulation Hypothesis raises philosophical challenges, such as questions about the nature of free will and the existence of an external reality. These challenges are not unique to The Simulation Hypothesis; they are also present in other philosophical frameworks such as solipsism and idealism. In the end, the Simulation Hypothesis provides a plausible explanation for the nature of reality that is consistent with our current understanding of physics and technology (Chalmers, 2016).

Overall, the evidence supporting the Simulation Hypothesis spans multiple disciplines, including physics, computer science and cognitive science. Quantum mechanics reveals phenomena such as superposition and entanglement, suggesting an underlying structure to reality that aligns with the concept of a programmed simulation. Advances in computational power, artificial intelligence and virtual reality have demonstrated the feasibility of creating highly detailed and realistic simulations, further supporting the hypothesis. Despite criticisms, such as the lack of direct evidence and the perceived computational limitations, The Simulation Hypothesis provides a comprehensive and logical explanation for the nature of reality. It accounts for the quantized nature of the universe and offers a plausible framework for understanding consciousness and perception. By addressing and debunking popular criticisms, we bolster the case for The Simulation Hypothesis, making it a robust and difficult-to-refute theory.

In fact, The Simulation Hypothesis may be the most complete and logical theory of existence available today. Unlike traditional religious and metaphysical explanations, it incorporates the latest advancements in science and technology providing the missing puzzle pieces of logic and fact that have eluded theologians and the ontologically inclined through the centuries. By integrating concepts from quantum mechanics, digital physics and artificial intelligence The Simulation Hypothesis offers a coherent and comprehensive explanation for the nature of our reality and, ironically, one that can be seen to embrace many concepts associated with what we might call the spiritual.

Philosophical Implications

Now we're really going deep into the fun parts! The very idea of The Simulation Hypothesis holds a vast number of implications, especially when it comes to questions about existence, consciousness and the true nature of reality. By exploring the concept from a variety of theoretical viewpoints and connecting them with the main precepts of The Simulation Hypothesis, we can deepen our understanding of how this theory intersects with and enriches both traditional and modern philosophical thinking.

Okay, okay; apologies in advance. I suggested that I was going to avoid Plato's Allegory of the Cave but I just can't help it. It turns out it is too tempting to refer to it when looking at classical philosophy. In this allegory prisoners are confined in a cave where they can only see shadows projected on the wall by objects behind them. The prisoners believe these shadows are all there is to reality until one breaks free and discovers the world, realizing that the shadows were reflections of a deeper reality (Plato, trans., 2008). The Simulation Hypothesis serves as a reflection of Plato's cave analogy by suggesting that our perceived reality might be akin to shadows or simulations of a profound underlying truth. Similar to how the cave prisoners were unaware of the real world, we too may be oblivious to the possibility that our reality is merely a simulation.

Throughout the centuries, advancements in technology and computing power have equipped us with the means to create and comprehend simulations, merging philosophical ideas with modern scientific concepts and capabilities. Plato's Allegory underscores the limits of perception and comprehension. The initial ignorance of the prisoners regarding the nature of reality mirrors our situation, where we may be unaware of living in a simulated world. The escaped prisoner symbolizes the philosopher or scientist who delves into truths about existence akin to how progress in physics and technology hints at the possibility of simulated realities. This connection implies that our quest for knowledge could eventually unveil the nature of our world in a similar manner to how the cave prisoner discovers life beyond his confinement.

George Berkeley's Idealism contemplated immaterialism or subjective idealism, asserting that reality is composed solely of minds and their perceptions. According to Berkeley, material objects exist only within perception; they manifest when observed by a conscious mind (Berkeley, 1710). The Simulation Hypothesis resonates with Berkeley's views by proposing that what we perceive as reality is potentially a construct experienced through our minds. If our world is indeed a simulation, it exists as information processed by our minds, thus aligning with Berkeley's belief that perception is the key to existence. As previously discussed, recent progress in neuroscience and cognitive science lends support to the notion that our perceptions and experiences are products of brain activity linking Berkeley's idealism with scientific knowledge. And, once again, we must consider this in terms of information being the consistent and ubiquitous denominator of our universe.

We can uncover similar alignment points within Friedrich Nietzsche's concept of eternal recurrence. Nietzsche introduced the idea of recurrence, suggesting that the universe and all its events repeat endlessly in a pattern; a notion that challenges individuals to seek purpose in their existence (Nietzsche, 1883). The Simulation Hypothesis contemplates an element of the challenge within eternal recurrence by proposing that our world could be one among numerous simulations possibly replayed with varying parameters. Nietzsche's theory of recurrence challenges us to seek meaning and direction in a cyclical existence. The Simulation Hypothesis extends this challenge by proposing that our world might be one version within a simulation, a perspective which prompts us to think about the consequences and importance of our actions in this world as well as the potential for growth and development across various versions. The technological progress facilitating the creation of simulations lends credence to this perspective, suggesting that our experiences and choices are part of an iterative process within a simulated realm.

The Mind Body Dilemma focuses on the connection between consciousness (the mind) and the physical realm (the body). Dualists argue for distinctness between mind and body while physicalists assert that consciousness emerges from processes in the brain (Chalmers, 1996). The Simulation Hypothesis offers a perspective on the relationship between the mind and body by proposing that consciousness and the physical world could both exist as components of a simulation. This idea supports physicalism by suggesting that consciousness is a result of information processing within this environment, yet it also introduces elements of dualism hinting at a distinction between the reality hosting the simulation and the simulated world.

The Matrix and Science Fiction as a Harbinger of Reality

Okay, let's step away from all the deep-thinking for a moment here and cover the topic of entertainment, such as movies and video games! Science fiction often serves as a precursor to real technological advancements and often provides a vision of the future that can inspire innovation and exploration. One of the most iconic representations of The Simulation Hypothesis in popular culture is the 1999 film *The Matrix*. In this film, humans live in a simulated reality created by intelligent machines with an aim to subdue the human population while their physical biological bodies are stored in vats. Although the premise of brains in vats might seem far-fetched, the underlying concept of a simulated reality is not entirely beyond the realm of possibility.

The Matrix explores themes of perception, control and the nature of reality echoing many of the philosophical questions raised by The Simulation Hypothesis. The film's depiction of a highly advanced simulation that is indistinguishable from reality resonates with current advancements in VR, AI and neuroscience. As we continue to develop technologies that can create increasingly immersive virtual environments and interface directly with the brain, the line between science fiction and reality seems to perpetually become ever more indistinguishable.

The influence of science fiction on technological development is well-documented. Concepts like space travel, artificial intelligence (and even the internet itself!) were once considered speculative fiction but have since become integral parts of our reality. This trend suggests that the ideas presented in *The Matrix* and similar works could one day materialize, driven by the same human curiosity and ingenuity that has propelled technological progress throughout history.

Jean Baudrillard, in *Simulacra and Simulation*, explores the nature of reality and hyperreality, arguing that "we live in a world where simulations have replaced reality to such an extent that the distinction between the real and the simulated has become almost meaningless" (Baudrillard, 1994). This notion aligns with the themes explored in *The Matrix* and reinforces the plausibility of living in a simulated reality.

I got into role playing adventure video games later in life and find them to be incredibly immersive, interactive and often fantastical experiences. The evolution of video games provides a glimpse into how interactive and immersive simulated environments can become. As a teenager, it was all 8-bit games like *Pacman* and *Galaga* and now I can spend hours exploring lands and interacting with other characters in worlds that seem as realistic as our own reality and universe. From simple pixelated graphics to lifelike 3D worlds, video games have advanced tremendously in the last few decades. Games like *Sims*, *Grand Theft Auto* and *Halo* offer vast, detailed worlds where players can interact with complex AI characters. As graphics continue to improve and AI becomes more sophisticated with links to haptics and virtual reality, these virtual environments will become even more realistic, potentially serving as precursors to full-scale simulations of reality.

With companies like Neuralink developing BCI's that could revolutionize how we interact with technology. These interfaces aim to create direct communication pathways between the brain and external devices, allowing for seamless integration with virtual environments. If successful, such technologies could enable users to experience virtual worlds as vividly as they do the physical world. The ability to upload and download experiences, memories and even consciousness could become a reality, laying the groundwork for highly immersive simulations.

Wrapping Up The Simulation Hypothesis

In this section we've looked deeply into the underpinning ideas of The Simulation Hypothesis. We've discussed its origins in both modern philosophies, its potential in technology and its links to neuroscience, quantum computing, VR and AI as they pertain to simulation. By examining this theory through the lenses of these disciplines we've set a strong groundwork for grasping the possibility of existing in a simulated world. This investigation not only prompts us to rethink our view of reality but it also paves the way for exploring and comprehending the essence of our existence.

PART THREE

Simularity - the Intersection of The Singularity and The Simulation Hypothesis

Well, we're here at an exciting and quirky crossroads: we've covered the concepts of both The Singularity and The Simulation Hypothesis. These groundbreaking ideas form a complex maze of potential outcomes for humanity as we approach the pivotal event of The Singularity. Throughout our exploration we have integrated numerous components spanning AI, philosophy, quantum physics, consciousness, technology and neuroscience. Each of these fields offers unique insights and evidence that collectively support the plausibility of these theories. AI and neuroscience illuminate the possibilities of creating conscious beings within a simulation, while quantum physics and philosophy provide frameworks for understanding the fundamental nature of reality. Together, these disciplines converge to form a comprehensive understanding of how a simulated reality could be constructed and maintained.

Now things are about to get interesting and unique. We hinted at the meeting point of The Singularity and The Simulation Hypothesis in the previous sections. It is in this forthcoming part where we'll delve deep into how they intersect. This isn't a thought experiment exercise: it is a probe into how these two concepts can come together to shape a fresh perspective on existence. By evaluating where they might connect, our goal is to create a narrative that raises thought-provoking queries that will push us to rethink the boundaries of our understanding and the essence of our world.

New Questions and Perspectives

Every decision we make is like a simple 'yes or no' choice between one thing or another (Virk, 2021). This idea reflects the statement by John Archibald Wheeler, known as 'It from bit' (Wheeler, 1990) which emphasizes that information forms the foundation of the universe. The notion that reality is essentially made up of information provides insights into how The Singularity might lead to the development of simulated worlds. As AI progresses towards superintelligence, it gains the ability to handle and generate profuse amounts of data giving rise to the ability to create more and more realistic simulations. These simulations go beyond replication of elements and environments; they also encompass the informational processes that underlie consciousness and perception. Physicist James Jeans captured this essence by stating that "the universe starts resembling an idea rather than a grand machine" (Jeans, 1930) highlighting the informational nature of reality.

Quantum mechanics also supports the notion that our reality is fundamentally rooted in information. The observer effect and experiments like delayed choice illustrate how our world appears to materialize from a range of outcomes when observed or measured. This occurrence can be seen as a type of real time processing of information, not at all dissimilar to how video game environments are rendered 'on-the-fly' and as needed for observation by the player. In this context, the potential of The Singularity is to deliver transformational tools that combine our human biology with unimaginable computational capacity and, in doing so, crafting and upholding simulations that mirror reality so closely that they are nearly impossible to distinguish from our everyday experiences. Virk encapsulates this idea by stating, "the fabric of our world is woven from information" (Virk, 2021) intertwining quantum mechanics principles with the framework of simulation.

John Wheeler's delayed choice experiment and the notion of 'It from bit', mentioned above, further integrate quantum physics and contemporary science with the concept of an informational universe. These theories suggest that information, rather than matter, forms the fundamental building blocks of reality. As physicist Anton Zeilinger states, "the distinction between reality and our knowledge of reality, between reality and information, cannot be made" (Bennet et al.,1993).

The convergence point between The Singularity and The Simulation Hypothesis is brought into focus through this lens of information as the fundamental constituent of our reality.

As we approach The Singularity, the advancements in technology and AI capabilities enable us to create complex simulations that go beyond replicating the external world. These simulations could also capture the experiences of consciousness giving rise to an infinite possible number and make-up of worlds and beings through information processing. Essentially, the concept of reality being reduced to information serves as a link between The Singularity and The Simulation Hypothesis. This viewpoint not only validates the possibility of constructing simulated realms but it also offers a structured approach to comprehend both the quantum mechanics and philosophical foundations that underpin our reality. By evaluating this intersection, we pave the way for inquiries and insights into unraveling the essence of our existence.

Philosophers like Daniel Dennett, who explores the concept of creating minds within powerful computing platforms (The Singularity) prompts a need for reconsidering the essence of consciousness and its corresponding connection to our perceptions of reality. Looking ahead, future philosophical discourse is likely to delve into the implications of living within realities. This exploration may involve pondering the distinctions between virtual experiences contemplating notions of will within predetermined simulations and examining how meaning and purpose can be constructed in artificial worlds (The Simulation Hypothesis). As our interactions with technologies become increasingly intertwined as we progress towards The Singularity, the boundaries between virtual realities are expected to become more indistinct fueling these ongoing philosophical discussions.

To tackle these emerging questions, philosophers must delve deeper into an interdisciplinary approach to fully gain a grasp on the implications of The Simularity Proposition. Philosopher Andy Clark suggests that the lines between humans and technology are blurring, urging a shift from classical designs to philosophies that focus on mind and cognition (Clark, 2003). By teaming up with technologists, scientists and philosophers we can help shape frameworks that steer the responsible incorporation of cutting-edge technologies in society. This collaboration is key to overcoming the challenges presented by the concept of The Simularity Proposition.

In the video "Exposing Scientific Dogmas - Banned TED Talk - Rupert Sheldrake," Rupert Sheldrake challenges our entrenched scientific dogmas, proposing that science should be more open to new ideas and paradigms. Sheldrake criticizes the rigid adherence to materialism and the belief that nature operates like a machine. He argues for a more holistic understanding of the universe, suggesting that it might be more accurately described in terms of information and consciousness rather than mere material interactions (Sheldrake, 2013). What is so fascinating is that this Ted Talk was banned on the basis that it was considered 'pseudoscience'. Now, eleven years later, many of the discoveries that have been uncovered in quantum physics, neuroscience and consciousness studies suggest that a second look at Sheldrake's proposal is necessary. While not all his suppositions would stand up to scrutiny, the rethinking of many of our scientific dogmas represents a point of view that is more reasonable as we take new learnings and consider them in terms of contemporary and emergent philosophy.

Connecting this to The Simularity, Sheldrake's arguments provide a foundation for the idea that the universe could be more about information than physical matter. As AI and technological advancements approach The Singularity, our understanding of reality could align more with The Simulation Hypothesis where the universe is perceived as a vast informational construct. This perspective challenges the traditional materialistic view, supporting the notion that our reality is fundamentally an intricate web of data and consciousness and aligning with the themes of The Simularity.

That this fundamentally challenges our conventional views on reality, consciousness and existence is not in question. Through examining these notions using idealism, materialism, dualism and informational ontology as perspectives, we can start to comprehend what it means to exist in a simulated realm. Looking ahead, philosophical exploration will be pivotal in delving into the epistemological and existential aspects of The Simularity Proposition to shape our understanding of human existence.

Historically, quantum mechanics has challenged classical deterministic views by introducing a probabilistic nature to physical processes. This shift from determinism to probability has profound implications for our understanding of reality. The Simulation Hypothesis leverages these quantum principles to suggest that reality itself could be a probabilistic simulation dynamically rendered based on informational inputs. The development from Planck's quantum hypothesis to Einstein's photoelectric effect and Schrödinger's wave mechanics reveals a gradual shift towards accepting that the fabric of reality is not entirely deterministic. This probabilistic nature forms a foundation for understanding how a simulated universe could operate, where outcomes within the context of The Singularity, are computed-based on probabilities rather than certainties.

As we have covered in the previous introductory sections, quantum computing represents a significant leap in computational power by utilizing the principles of quantum mechanics. Quantum bits, or qubits, can exist in multiple states simultaneously, enabling quantum computers to process vast amounts of information more efficiently than classical computers. This technological advancement supports the feasibility of creating and maintaining complex simulations. As physicist David Deutsch notes, "Quantum computation... will be the first technology that allows useful tasks to be performed in collaboration between parallel universes" (Deutsch, 1997). The emergence of AI-powered VR and AR technologies reinforces this trajectory. These innovations offer experiences that challenge our understanding of reality and expand opportunities for human innovation and engagement. According to technologist Kevin Kelly's observation; "The digital realm will be as impactful as the world seamlessly integrating into our routines." (Kelly, 2016).

As we edge closer to The Singularity, the ability for AI to craft and engage with states within multiple universe simulations moves from being merely possible to becoming inevitable. Advanced artificial intelligence and computing technologies will empower us to create universes with each offering distinct experiences and chances for discovery. The Simularity Proposition symbolizes the peak of this transformation, where human thinking merges with computer systems, enabling us to experience and exist in multiverse simulations. In such a world, the lines between what's virtual and what's physical disintegrates as both are expressions of the underlying information foundation.

This shift in perspective is also backed by physicist Anton Zeilinger, who argued that "the boundary between reality and our understanding of reality between reality and data is indistinguishable" (Zeilinger, 2010). Zeilinger's ideas highlight the interconnectedness of what we perceive as reality with the information that shapes it. With advancements in technology that will arrive with The Simularity, we can increasingly manipulate this information to construct realities bridging the gap between knowledge and existence.

As Marshall McLuhan famously expressed in 1964, "we shape our tools and thereafter our tools shape us" (McLuhan,1964) highlighting the relationship between humans and technology that is essential for grasping the potential implications of The Simularity. With each leap, our way of life, work dynamics and perception of reality undergo transformations setting off a cycle of continuous innovation and adaptation. In this way, the progress of humanity has always been closely linked with technological advancement. From inventions like the wheel to innovations such as internet technology, these developments have played a pivotal role in shaping societies and economies. In the realm of The Simularity Proposition, technology not only facilitates the creation of simulations but it also propels the exponential growth foreseen by The Singularity concept.

In the video "New Evidence For The Simulation Hypothesis? Donald Hoffman on The Simulation Argument," Donald Hoffman explores the notion that our reality might be a sophisticated simulation. He posits that our sensory experiences and the material world are merely evolved interfaces designed for survival and not for uncovering objective truth. Drawing from quantum mechanics and cognitive science, Hoffman suggests that our perceptions are akin to a user interface that obscures the true nature of existence. Hoffman argues convincingly that our brains simplify and interpret complex data into survival-oriented information, creating an 'interface' that may not accurately reflect reality. Using analogies like computer desktops and icons, he illustrates how our perceptions might be symbolic representations of more profound underlying processes (Hoffman, 2023).

Linking this to The Simularity Proposition, Hoffman's ideas imply that The Singularity event could significantly alter our understanding of the universe. As AI and technology advance, they might reveal that our reality aligns more with a simulated framework rather than a purely materialistic and deterministic one. This perspective supports The Simularity premise that approaching this tipping point will increasingly align our understanding of existence with simulation theories and thereby challenging conventional views of reality.

The Crucial Interplay between AI and Consciousness within The Simularity Proposition

Artificial Intelligence plays a progressively instrumental role in the study of consciousness. Recent advancements in AI have not only transformed countless fields of scientific inquiry but have also introduced new tools and frameworks for exploring consciousness.

We've covered the fact that over the past few decades there have been remarkable breakthroughs in artificial intelligence, especially in areas like machine learning, neural networks and natural language processing. These advancements empower AI systems to carry out tasks once believed to be an exclusive domain only within the grasp of human intelligence such as speech recognition, language comprehension and even cognitive processing abilities. A particularly significant recent milestone is the rise of deep learning technology, which utilizes layered neural networks to analyze intricate data patterns. Deep learning mirrors how the human brain learns from experience and equips AI systems to enhance their performance over time without the need for intervention through programming.

These advanced technology-based learning methods can be credited to AI's capacity to manage extensive volumes of data and recognize complex patterns that often surpass human capabilities. As a result, AI systems have been created that can outperform humans in tasks. For example, AlphaGo, created by DeepMind defeated the world champion Go player showcasing AI's potential to excel in strategic games. Go, a game known for its complexity and vast outcome possibilities had long posed a challenge for AI. According to David Silver "The victory was not only a breakthrough in Go's history, also in the field of AI itself demonstrating the effectiveness of reinforcement learning and neural networks" (Silver et al., 2016). AlphaGo's triumph was made possible through a mix of learning where it was trained on a set of human Go games with specialized reinforcement learning. It competed against itself in millions of games to enhance its strategies. This combined approach enabled AlphaGo to develop tactics and insights that even top human players had not uncovered. This significant advancement has very far-reaching implications for AI research indicating that similar methods could be utilized in fields that require strategic thinking and problem-solving skills. Was it conscious of its win? Probably not. But could it be in the not-too-distant future? Absolutely.

When contemplated in consideration of the fact that the focus of AI research has increasingly shifted towards comprehending and imitating elements of consciousness, it becomes clear that machine consciousness will ultimately come to fruition. This avenue of exploration aims to uncover the mysteries surrounding the emergence of experiences from activities and how they can be emulated or simulated by artificial systems. In her book *Consciousness; An Introduction,* Susan Blackmore emphasizes the potential of AI in illuminating the mechanisms behind conscious experiences. She suggests that AI provides a doorway through which to delve into the enigmas of consciousness, offering both insights and practical applications. One promising area where AI has made strides in comprehending consciousness is through crafting network models that mimic aspects of human cognitive functions. These models strive to mirror the brain's operations by replicating the structure and behavior of circuits. For instance, convolutional neural networks (CNNs) have demonstrated success in visual recognition tasks closely resembling how the visual cortex processes information. This progress has enhanced our understanding of visual perception mechanisms and their potential replication in quantum computational systems (Blackmore, 2005).

AI's capacity to analyze voluminous datasets has paved the way for exploring consciousness in learning and generative models that empower AI systems to recognize patterns and produce data that mirrors human creativity and intuition. For instance. generative adversarial networks (GANs) have been employed to produce images, music and text demonstrating AI's potential to mimic human creative abilities (Blackmore, 2005). This talent for generating content raises thought-provoking inquiries about the essence of creativity and its connection to consciousness.

Beyond simulating functions, AI has also played a pivotal role in enhancing our comprehension of the neural underpinnings of consciousness. Combining neuroimaging techniques with machine learning algorithms has enabled researchers to interpret brain activity and forecast states of mind with improved precision. By studying how the brain functions in these ways, artificial intelligence can assist in recognizing the brain patterns linked to states of awareness such as being awake, asleep or experiencing altered states induced by certain practices like meditation or ingesting substances like psychedelics.

Without question, the capability of AI to perform tasks involving perception, learning and decision-making inherently serves to challenge many of our established beliefs about consciousness. If AI systems can imitate or surpass these fundamental human capabilities, it naturally prompts questions into the essence of consciousness and whether it emerges from complex information processing. This view resonates with cognitive scientist Anil Seth's perspective that consciousness originates from the coding mechanisms within the brain. In his book *Being You; A New Science of Consciousness*, Seth discusses how the brain acts as a predictor constantly forming and adjusting a picture of the world based on what we perceive. This process of predicting and correcting errors is crucial for our sense of consciousness and AI models that imitate these functions offer insights into how consciousness could arise from brain processes (Seth, 2021).

This integration of AI in studying consciousness carries significant implications for The Simularity Proposition in that, as AI systems grow more advanced, they possess the capacity needed to generate simulations capable of mimicking conscious experiences. A core principle at the heart of this theory is the utilization of AI in shaping the boundaries between physical realms. Within this context there is a hypothesis that consciousness itself could stem from similar underlying conditions and mechanisms that are indistinguishable whether they are organic or artificial.

Erich Neumann delves into the evolution of awareness from the perspectives of mythology and psychology in *The Origins and History of Consciousness*. According to Neumann's findings, the emergence of artificial consciousness prompts a reevaluation of the origins and essence of self-transcending paradigms (Neumann, 1954). In addition, examining how AI impacts the evolution of consciousness reveals a connection between theories on cognitive evolution and our understanding of consciousness development over time. These potential implications of AI-driven consciousness are profound. If it is possible to simulate consciousness it opens the possibility that our reality can be defined through simulations created by superintelligent AI systems. This idea aligns with Richard Dawkins' exploration in *The Selfish Gene*, where he investigates concepts such as replicators and information's role in evolution and suggests that the notion of replicating consciousness through non-human computational processes supports the idea that our reality could indeed be a simulation (Dawkins, 1976).

An interrelated consideration revolves around the capability to create simulations leading to challenges with respect to our understanding of identity and self. Neumann discusses this topic in *The Origins and History of Consciousness,* examining how individual consciousness evolves through psychological perspectives through which his research implies that the possibility of machine-produced consciousness and prompts us to reassess the idea of identity surpassing conventional biological frameworks (Neumann, 1954). If an intelligent AI can create one simulation it makes sense that it could produce multiple simulations, each with their own distinct settings and outcomes. This notion aligns with theories in physics regarding multiverses and suggests the existence of universes governed by variegated and infinite possibilities in terms of physical laws and constants. The capacity to simulate consciousness across realities poses questions about free will's nature, the continuity of one's identity and the purpose behind existence.

We took at Musser's insights in the previous section. His findings propose that consciousness is not a product of brain activity but a fundamental element intertwined within the quantum fabric. By drawing on insights from physicists and philosophers like David Bohm and Roger Penrose, he explores how quantum processes may play a role in shaping experiences. This scope of inquiry is in line with theories suggesting that the brain operates as a quantum system and processes information in ways that classical physics cannot fully explain. Musser highlights the potential of AI to revolutionize our grasp of consciousness. Through simulating processes and analyzing vast data sets, AI has the capacity to uncover some of the most profound mysteries surrounding human thought and the universe (Musser, 2021).

Another prominent duo in this space, Menas Kafatos and Robert Nadeau, also propose that consciousness and the universe are intertwined. In their publication, *The Conscious Universe: Parts and Wholes in Physical Reality* the authors postulate that consciousness is an integral element of the cosmos, bridging the divide between quantum mechanics and classical physics. They highlight the importance of the observer in shaping reality in line with Musser's view on how all phenomena are interconnected (Kafatos and Nadeau, 2000). And, lastly, Philosopher Philip Goff champions a form of panpsychism asserting that consciousness is an aspect of all entities. Goffs' ideas challenge many commonly held beliefs by proposing that consciousness could be as fundamental as space and time. This stance resonates with the quantum perspective which views consciousness as an omnipresent element in the cosmos (Goff, 2019).

If consciousness is truly a quantum phenomenon, merging AI with human minds might involve utilizing quantum processes that could result in advancements in cognitive abilities (a definite possibility through The Singularity). If consciousness functions on a quantum scale it suggests that our simulated world follows quantum principles, thereby altering the boundaries between what is simulated and what is genuine from our unique human perspective.

In terms of The Simularity Proposition and the factor of simulated reality, AI's role in this hypothesis is twofold: it helps in the theoretical exploration of simulation concepts and provides practical methodologies for assessing these ideas. For instance, AI algorithms have been employed to detect patterns in cosmic background radiation that might indicate artificial manipulation, suggesting possible signs of a simulated universe (Gough, 2020). This pattern recognition capability is crucial as it allows researchers to sift through vast amounts of data for anomalies that might indicate simulation artifacts. In addition to cosmic background radiation, AI has been used to analyze large-scale structures in the universe. By comparing observed data with simulated models, researchers can identify discrepancies that might suggest a simulated origin. This approach leverages AI's ability to model complex systems and detect subtle deviations that human observers might miss. Scholars like Rizwan Virk have explored how AI and gaming technology can create immersive simulated experiences, providing a framework for considering The Simulation Hypothesis and, by extension, The Simularity Proposition

(Virk, 2021). The quantum aspect of consciousness implies that our cognitive functions are deeply entwined with the essence of the universe whether it is natural or artificial and this interconnectedness might hold the key to unlocking insights into the nature of our reality. Through blending these ideas from quantum physics, artificial intelligence and philosophical exploration, The Simularity Proposition offers a theory that tackles the core queries of existence. This method does not just push the boundaries of understanding but it also presents fresh perspectives on human identity in a world that grows ever more intricate and interconnected. As we will look at in the following section, this leads us to a path of inquiry that gets to the core questions of our existence.

Questions of Existence: Why Are We Here?

As sentient creatures, we humans possess a capacity for contemplating perplexing questions about our reality. This unique ability to ponder our existence, the significance of life itself and our own mortality distinguishes us (at least to the extent of our current knowledge) from other life forms.

Our comprehension of the universe has undergone transformations over time starting from the observations made by ancient societies. Ancient civilizations interpreted the cosmos through myths and superstitions creating stories to make sense of the events they witnessed. As our understanding and instruments progressed, so did our grasp of how the universe is structured and designed. The transition from myth to science took shape with the contributions of thinkers who introduced models of the universe. Intellectuals like Ptolemy advocated for models that positioned Earth at the center of all things. These concepts held sway for centuries until a new phase of exploration emerged during the Renaissance period. Influential figures such as Copernicus, Galileo and Kepler reshaped our understanding by proving that Earth revolves around the Sun, and in doing so challenged established beliefs and setting the foundation for astronomy. The invention of telescopes empowered Galileo to make groundbreaking discoveries; he uncovered Jupiter's moons and observed Venus' changing phases. These findings offered proof in favor of the sun-centered model while questioning the earth-centered belief. Galileo's contributions then set the stage for Isaac Newton, whose principles of motion and gravity established a foundation for comprehending dynamics (Sobel, 2011). Newton's seminal work, *Principia Mathematica* released in 1687 outlined the laws of motion and gravity presenting a background for studying body movements (Newton, 1999 trans 1687). This marked a departure from interpretations of the universe by anchoring our knowledge in empirical observations.

Albert Einstein's Theory of Relativity again offered insights that ultimately reshaped our perceptions of space and time. His equations demonstrated that gravity is not merely a force but rather a bending of spacetime caused by objects. This shift in perspective fundamentally transformed our outlook on the cosmos and gave rise to cosmology as a field (Einstein, 1916). Then, the groundbreaking discovery made by Edwin Hubble regarding an expanding universe further transmuted our understanding; it indicated that the universe is dynamic and continuously evolving. The Big Bang theory gained prominence as the explanation for how the universe began, depicting a powerful event that led to the creation of all matter and energy (Hubble, 1929). This idea has been backed by scientific observations such as the cosmic microwave background radiation which is viewed as the lingering effects of the Big Bang (Until now - as we will touch upon after just one more paragraph, even *it* has now come under skepticism).

In more recent decades, technological advancements have enabled us to peer even deeper into the universe's most profound mysteries. The identification of matter and dark energy (substances that make up most of the universe's mass energy but remain unseen and not well understood) has opened new horizons in cosmology. These findings again contradict and challenge our existing knowledge and propose that we may only grasp a fraction of what makes up the universe. Our comprehension and perception of how the universe is organized is evolving with each insight brought about by technological progress.

For instance, although the Big Bang Theory has long been considered the guiding and widely accepted concept in cosmology, fresh discoveries have started to emerge that bring with them new doubts. Roger Penrose, a physicist who received a Nobel Prize proposed a compelling idea about the universe not being an occurrence. His theory of Conformal Cyclic Cosmology (CCC) suggests that the universe experiences cycles of bangs and subsequent contractions. Penrose points to patterns in the Cosmic Microwave Background (CMB) radiation as remnants from a prior universe challenging the traditional belief that the Big Bang initiated everything. This revolutionary concept implies that our current universe is one phase in a series of cosmic eras and shifts our perspective from viewing history as linear to seeing it as cyclical indicating that the universe rejuvenates itself over stretches of time. Penrose's theory highlights how scientific knowledge continually evolves and lends further credence to The Simularity Proposition in that we are still in the process of continuously unearthing the true nature of our reality.

As we venture further into the cosmos it is crucial to embrace emerging concepts and be open to revising our comprehension based on these evolving insights. A recent feature in BBC Science Focus Magazine titled "Challenges with Our Understanding of the Universe; Unraveling Mysteries", embodies this pursuit of knowledge. It sheds light on the anomalies and enigmas that endure within our frameworks and suggests the need for new theories and approaches to make sense of these discoveries (BBC Science Focus, 2024).

As we approach, or perhaps are already in, The Singularity era, our ideas in how we perceive and understand the cosmos and our place in it will inevitably continue to shift and develop.

The Meaning of Life and Death

Throughout history humans have pondered the meaning of life and the mysteries of death with curiosity. Different cultures and time periods have produced ideas and beliefs to comprehend these aspects of our existence. From mythical tales to philosophies our thoughts on life and death have influenced how we see the world, our faiths and our societies.

Many societies viewed life and death through a largely mythical perspective. For example, the ancient Egyptians believed in an afterlife journey to the underworld. They took care in preserving bodies through mummification because they thought it was essential for the soul's survival after death (Hornung, 1999). Similarly, the Greeks and Romans had their polygamous gods and intricate beliefs about what happens after death - souls finding peace in Elysium while the wicked faced punishment in Tartarus.

Religion has been instrumental in shaping how we perceive life and death. The major world religions offer teachings about what comes after this life. In Christianity, heaven and hell serve as guidelines offering rewards or punishments based on one's actions during their lifetime. Hinduism and Buddhism contrastingly focus on the idea of rebirth and karma where one's deeds in this lifetime influence the circumstances of next lives. These spiritual viewpoints not only provide solace in the presence of death but have also served as a moral guide for their followers. They give significance to life by suggesting that our actions carry repercussions that transcend our physical being in this existence. This fusion of ethics and mortality has deeply shaped our customs and conduct over time.

Distinct from religious convictions, various philosophical doctrines have endeavored to unravel the enigmas of existence and demise. Existentialist thinkers like Søren Kierkegaard and Jean Paul Sartre wrestled with the lack of meaning in life within a universe of divine intention. They contended that individuals must forge their purpose through choices and behaviors (Sartre, 1946).

Over time, scientific progress has often been found to be contradictory to these historical interpretations around the meaning of life. For instance, neuroscience has delved into the foundations of consciousness and how the brain actually shapes our perceptions of life and death. These captivating fields of investigation focus on understanding consciousness in the realms of life and death. Progress in neuroscience has shed light on how the brain's intricate neural connections give rise to thoughts, feelings and self-awareness and this leads to implications for our comprehension of mortality, especially regarding what happens to consciousness beyond the body's survival. The intriguing phenomenon of near-death experiences, where individuals describe transformative encounters while clinically deceased, has ignited discussions about the essence of consciousness and its potential continuity after death (Greyson, 2003).

Within The Simularity Proposition, death might be viewed as a transition to another form of being where our knowledge continues to have an impact and where our consciousness can essentially be uploaded and downloaded into new simulated realities. This perspective is in line with the principles of transhumanism which promote the use of technology to surpass the limitations of our biology and explore different realms of existence (Bostrom, 2005).

When we consider the ideas of The Singularity and The Simulation Hypothesis together, and in doing so forming the basis of The Simularity Proposition, we can see how they complement each other. The technological progress anticipated by The Singularity is crucial for bringing The Simulation Hypothesis into fruition and without these advancements, the concept of creating a simulation as vast as a universe would be unattainable. Therefore, The Singularity acts as a precursor for gaining insights and potentially confirming The Simulation Hypothesis. This is the tipping point for The Simularity Proposition where this intersection brings about advancing technology that will lead us to profound new understandings about our existence. It proposes that what we traditionally think of as a soul could be transferred (like information) across realities or simulations. This viewpoint resonates with theories that consider information to be a fundamental element of our universe as argued by researchers such as Vlatko Vedral. If we could somehow keep our consciousness intact and move it around it would really shake up how we think about the laws of nature, religion and who we are as individuals (Vedral, 2010).

A fascinating new supposition has recently come into play on this subject. The theory, as explained in a 2022 video article by Neural Networks entitled *The Terrifying Quantum Theory Scientists Don't Even Want to Talk About,* examines a perplexing quantum theory called Quantum Suicide and Immortality, a thought experiment related to Schrödinger's Cat. It suggests that in a scenario where a person's life depends on a quantum event, the person will never experience their death, only alternate realities where they survive in perpetuity. This raises philosophical questions about consciousness and the nature of reality, challenging our understanding of life and death (Neural Networks, 2022).

Quantum Suicide implies that every time a quantum decision is made, the universe splits, creating a multiverse where every possible outcome happens. This theory suggests that our consciousness might continue in a branch of the universe where we survive, leading to the idea of subjective immortality. It is a controversial and unsettling concept, implying endless continuity of consciousness despite the occurrence of potentially fatal events. There are crucial implications to this theory related to free will and determinism, questioning whether our choices are truly our own or determined by quantum probabilities. It explores how this thought experiment intersects with interpretations of quantum mechanics, like the Many-Worlds Interpretation and its potential to redefine our understanding of existence and the fabric of the universe.

Thinking about life and death forces us to question what really matters to us. If everything we know is part of a simulation what do our choices mean? Does it change how important our experiences and relationships are to us? These are not just musings to peruse and ponder; they have real world implications for how we lead our lives and connect with others and, consequently, need to be contemplated with the gravitas the subject warrants.

In the end, figuring out the meaning of life and facing the concept of death is no rudimentary task. With technology advancing ideas like The Simularity Proposition, it proffers upon us new ways to tackle these timeless mysteries. The idea that there might be more to learn through simulations suggests that our quest for understanding is far from finished and that future breakthroughs will keep reshaping how we see life, death and existence. This is the crux of The Simularity Proposition: that the impending Singularity will be an unprecedented event in human evolution, characterized by an explosion of possibilities and transformative experiences. As we reach this convergence, it will become evident that our world is fundamentally composed of information and our grasp of the universe is still elementary. The Simularity envisions a future where we possess the capability to create new simulations and realities, leveraging the advancements brought forth by The Singularity. This synthesis not only redefines our perception of reality but also unlocks the potential to explore and inhabit myriad new dimensions of existence. It is also an ideal set up for the next area of discussion: more fun and puzzling thoughts about religion and spirituality and how we deal with these in the light of The Simularity (because it cannot really be a 'new' world view if it doesn't promote us replacing the old ones).

PART FOUR

The Crossroads of Religious Faith, Spirituality and The Simularity

In the preceding portions of this essay, we ventured into our universe, existence and humanity's place within this vast cosmic framework. We dissected the intricacies of reality, inquiring into the nature of the universe and the fundamental questions surrounding our existence. These discussions have laid a robust foundation for understanding the theoretical underpinnings of The Simularity Proposition. Now, as we progress to the next segment of our exploration, we tread into an area that, while deeply connected with human experience, is often considered delicate and highly personal: the domain of faith, spirituality and religion. So, why not? Let's jump right in!

Addressing the intersection of spirituality and The Simularity is not just an academic exercise; it is an imperative. Faith and spirituality have long been cornerstones of human civilization, shaping cultures, moral frameworks and individual identities. To leave this critical aspect untouched would result in an incomplete and superficial understanding of our quest to reconcile The Simularity Proposition with the full spectrum of human experience. By examining this, we can construct a more comprehensive and holistic perspective that respects the significance of spirituality in human life while offering a compelling alternative rationalization through the lens of The Simularity.

This chapter may be perceived as more sensitive as it directly engages with deeply held beliefs and values. However, the goal is not to challenge or diminish these beliefs (well, maybe a little) but to expand the dialogue, exploring how The Simularity deals with and even maybe enriches spiritual understanding. The potential of this to offer new insights into age-old spiritual questions presents an exciting frontier for both philosophical and theological discourse.

First, we will trace the history and background of our predominant religions.

Evolution of World Religions

Throughout history, spirituality has played a role in our lives, offering explanations and different answers to life's deepest questions and quandaries. Early humans grappled with their existence in the world and the concept of life and death. Spirituality provided our ancestors with a channel through which they could make sense of these aspects of existence and bring solace and a feeling of connection to something bigger and more profound than themselves. This innate quest for meaning and comprehension is fundamental to our nature, as noted by psychologist Carl Jung who believed that living without purpose is unbearable (Jung, 1961).

As societies progressed from groups to communities, the importance of social cohesion became necessary. According to Yuval Noah Harari in *Sapiens; A History of Humankind*, humans have an innate tendency or need to form social bonds. Maintaining these bonds becomes challenging when groups grow beyond 150 individuals unless they share beliefs and stories. Harari suggests that at this scale, human cooperation relies on shared myths that exist within our collective imagination (Harari, 2015). Myths and beliefs have served as the fabric that binds communities together, enabling them to function efficiently and ultimately leading to the formation of organized religions. Over time, individual spiritual inclinations evolved into faith systems that were shaped by geographical and historical influences resulting in a diverse array of belief systems. Despite their variations, major religions share an objective; they aim to unravel the mysteries of life, offer ethical principles and cultivate a sense of belonging among their adherents.

Advancements in neuroscience and the exploration of consciousness have provided insights into humanity's inclination towards spirituality. Studies suggest that our brains are inherently predisposed to metaphysical encounters and beliefs, indicating that something about spirituality is ingrained in cognition. This research has revealed that specific brain regions like the cortex and parietal lobes become active during religious experiences and that these areas are linked to self-transcendence; a state where individuals feel connected to something greater and more profound than themselves. Neuroscientist Andrew Newberg has conducted extensive studies on how the brain contributes to these spiritual encounters. In his book *How God Changes Your Brain*, Newberg discusses how engaging in ritualized religious practices can bring about lasting changes in various brain structures and functions, ultimately influencing one's values and perception of reality. These transformations have the potential to foster compassion, empathy and overall psychological wellbeing suggesting that spirituality not only occurs naturally but also contributes positively to overall health (Newberg, 2009).

Further research conducted by Newberg and d'Aquili on the neuropsychology of these experiences indicates that the brain's default mode network (DMN) plays a role in shaping spiritual encounters. The DMN becomes active when individuals are in a state of rest and internally focused on introspection and self-referential thinking. During activities such as meditation or prayer, alterations in DMN activity patterns give rise to sensations of unity, timelessness, and a diminished sense of self. This neurological foundation for such encounters highlights the relationship between brain function and spirituality (d'Aquili and Newberg, 1999). Additionally, significant insights have emerged from studies on 'neurotheology,' which investigate the interplay between the brain and religious occurrences. Neuroscientist John Horgan defines neurotheology as an avenue for comprehending human beings' seemingly common inclinations toward spirituality. He mentions that our brains appear to be naturally inclined towards religious or spiritual events, having evolved over millennia to foster unity and collaboration within communities (Horgan, 2018). This viewpoint coincides with Harari's observation that stories and convictions play an indispensable role in upholding social groups.

With advancing comprehension and studies in the discipline of human consciousness it is increasingly evident that spirituality is a fundamental (not fundamentalist!) aspect of our makeup. The formalization of spirituality into religions can be viewed as a progression, where shared beliefs and rituals offer organization and coherence in expansive societies. This institutionalization establishes regulations, norms and guiding principles that aid in sustaining unity and advancing welfare. Harari's insights accentuate the importance of these frameworks for the functioning of societies, connecting spiritualism with the entrenched faith systems that have influenced human civilization.

The prominent global religions have significantly impacted our history, our customs, and our ideologies. Each faith tradition, though distinct in its teachings and customs, presents an array of beliefs and practices reflecting humanity's approaches to grasping divine concepts.

Hinduism stands as one of the oldest known organized religions; its roots trace back to 1500 BCE on the Indian subcontinent. Various beliefs and practices are encompassed in Hinduism, including ideas such as reincarnation, karma, and dharma. In Hinduism, a diverse array of deities are conceived, with Brahman representing reality and highlighting the acceptance of paths to spiritual enlightenment. The Bhagavad Gita, a Hindu scripture, conveys the message that all paths taken by individuals ultimately lead to the virtuous path.

Buddhism originated in the sixth century BCE, borne from Hinduism and was established by Siddhartha Gautama, known as the Buddha. It revolves around the Four Truths and the Eightfold Path as a means to attaining enlightenment through meditation, ethical behavior and wisdom. Unlike Hinduism's emphasis on deity worship, Buddhism directs attention toward an individual's quest for awakening.

Judaism stands out as one of the oldest faiths with its roots tracing back to ancient Hebrews. Central to Judaism is belief in an all-powerful deity who established a special covenant with the Jewish people. The Torah, which is the central text of Judaism, provides guidelines and teachings that shape the spiritual aspects of the lives of its followers. As a believed fulfilment of Judaism's promise of a Messiah, Christianity originated in the first century AD and was centered around the life and lessons of Jesus. Christians affirm that Jesus is God's Son and the redeemer of humanity, offering salvation through his crucifixion and resurrection to all who have faith. The Bible consists of the Old and New Testaments and serves as Christianity's scripture. Jesus' teachings underscore love, compassion and forgiveness epitomized by his words 'love your neighbor as yourself.'

Of the major world religions, Islam is the most recent faith tradition having been established in the seventh century AD by Prophet Muhammad on the belief in one God, Allah. The Quran serves as Islam's scripture. Muslims adhere to the Five Pillars of Islam as practices and beliefs to their faith including bearing witness, to faith, prayer, giving alms, fasting during Ramadan and undertaking pilgrimage.

These various major religions each contain their unique beliefs and customs, however, they share key threads in their principal teachings and objectives. As Karen Armstrong points out in her book *The Case, for God*, religious doctrines and practices are intended not for knowledge but also to cultivate a specific internal disposition (Armstrong, 2009). While these various faiths have their distinctions, they often share perspectives on the universe such as the collective belief in an afterlife of various forms or a supreme being overseeing all existence. These common aspects indicate a tendency to search for meaning, purpose and connection through spirituality and belief. For example, Hinduism's idea of rebirth and Christianity's concept of the afterlife, both demonstrate a common interest in what happens to the soul after death.

The progression of religions from spiritual customs to intricate belief systems highlights how human spirituality adapts over time. Each religion, though unique in its practices and nuanced belief systems, fulfills the human desire to comprehend existence and discover belonging and purpose within a broader context. As Huston Smith expresses in *The World's Religions*, "when we consider the world's enduring faiths, at their finest we encounter the wisdom of humanity" (Smith, 1991).

As we approach The Singularity. the rapid progress of technology holds the promise of reshaping every facet of existence including our religious encounters. The fusion of intelligence, biotechnology and quantum computing stands to enrich our comprehension of the cosmos and our position within it. In this milieu, established faiths may discover significance and resonance as the revelations from technology's progress deepen our grasp of spiritual doctrines and moral lessons. And, of course, our exponentially advancing knowledge may bring about contradictions that will serve as ideas that dispute the basic premises upon which these religious beliefs rest. The nearing Singularity prompts us to reassess the groundworks of our belief systems, contemplating how emerging technologies could offer novel viewpoints on timeless inquiries. By examining the wisdom of The Simularity Proposition against a backdrop of religious beliefs and explanations, we find ourselves in a position to shape a rounded perspective that values and enriches the naturally occurring spiritual aspect of human life. With an open-minded approach, this examination can lead to coherent and convincing insights into these facets of human existence and bridge the gap between scientific knowledge and spirituality in a transformative manner.

Spiritual interpretations of events, existence and the universe have significantly influenced how humans perceive life and the cosmos. However, they often lack a comprehensive understanding. One key drawback is their reliance on scriptures and doctrines which, though abundant in their teachings, may not fully address the complexities and facts associated with established modern scientific views on the universe. With advancements in cosmology, physics and neuroscience expanding our understanding, religious narratives are increasingly under scrutiny. And, of course, let's face it, throughout history religion and science have frequently clashed. The dispute between Galileo and the Catholic Church regarding heliocentrism serves as an illustration of this conflict. Galileo's findings supported the theory that positioned the sun at the center of our solar system which was in direct conflict with the Church's geocentric belief system. This confrontation underscored the contradiction between faith-driven perspectives and those based on evidence. As science advanced it continued to challenge standing interpretations leading to what Stephen Jay Gould termed as "non overlapping magisteria" (NOMA), the concept that science and religion have distinct and separate areas of authority (Gould, 1997).

In many respects, this divide presents individuals with a choice: faith or fact? Traditional religions often require belief without evidence, emphasizing faith as an aspect of spiritual life. On the opposite side of the equation, science depends on testable and repeatable phenomena to construct knowledge. This contrast can create discord for those seeking to harmonize their beliefs with scientific insights. Consequently, some individuals may find themselves torn between their faith and acceptance of established truths, decision-points that can evoke strong polarization. Debates surrounding issues like evolution, climate change and medical ethics serve as modern day exemplars of the enduring conflict between beliefs and scientific viewpoints. Richard Dawkins, in *The God Delusion*, suggests that faith can sometimes be used to avoid spiritual contemplation while simultaneously disregarding evidence that brings into question believers' comfort-based belief systems: "faith can sometimes be used as a way to avoid existential thinking" (Dawkins, 2006).

The emergence of atheism led by figures like Dawkins, Christopher Hitchens and Sam Harris emphasizes the widening gap between faith-based beliefs and empirical evidence. These thinkers argue that religion lacks necessity and, even more critically, could also pose risks in light of progress. As expressed by Sam Harris in *The End of Faith*, there is a conflict between religion and science where advancements in one often come at the expense of the other. This conflicting perspective reflects the challenge individuals face when trying to find harmony between these opposing realms of thought (Harris, 2004).

Looking ahead to next era which will be marked by continued advancements in capabilities and accelerated knowledge, a potential for a more unified comprehension arises. The Simularity Proposition, as we have articulated, signifies a juncture where human intelligence merges with machine intelligence, potentially leading to insights into the essence of reality and consciousness. This scenario presents an increasing likelihood of bridging the gap between beliefs and scientific endeavors. The fusion of spirituality with inquiry goes beyond theoretical speculation; it becomes imperative for achieving a comprehensive understanding of existence as a whole. Spirituality caters to our innate human need for significance, connection and direction while science equips us with tools and methodologies to delve into the mysteries of the physical universe. By combining these viewpoints, we can form an outlook that respects our spiritual desires while also embracing the rational and evidence-based progress of science. The new discoveries in comprehending consciousness further demonstrate the potential for a connection between spirituality and science. The examination of consciousness within the realm of philosophy and spirituality has now become a focal point of scientific exploration.

Theoretical physicist Michio Kaku proposes in his work *The Future of the Mind* that through the fusion of neuroscience and technology we may unravel the aspects of our minds potentially leading to a comprehension of our spiritual encounters (Kaku, 2014). Kaku's perspective underscores the potential for a relationship between spirituality and science where each realm enriches and enlightens the other.

The limitations of interpretations alongside historical divergences between faith and science emphasize the necessity for a fresh approach. This proposal suggests a way that respects the depth of spirituality while also embracing the thorough exploration of scientific knowledge leading to a broader perspective on the cosmos and our role in it. Ultimately, this will entail a move away from our historical understandings and belief systems as they pertain to institutional, faith-based religions (of course, given some of our other 'innate human' tendencies, it will likely take a very, very, very, very long time before *everyone* comes along for this ride of enlightenment!).

The Outdated Nature of World Religions

In our contemporary world, the traditional narratives offered by world religions increasingly appear outdated and inadequate for addressing the profound questions about the meaning of life. While religions have historically provided comfort and a framework for understanding our existence, they often rely on ancient texts and doctrines that do not align with our current scientific knowledge and technological capabilities. These belief systems, rooted in the philosophical musings of prophets and believers who lived in primitive conditions with limited knowledge and perspective beyond their immediate world experience, lack the logical coherence necessary to satisfy the intellectual demands of modern society.

The philosophical foundations of most world religions were established in eras when human understanding of the universe was extremely limited. Prophets and religious founders lived in times when the cosmos was a mystery, psychology was non-existent and historical narratives were passed down through oral traditions. In *Sapiens: A Brief History of Humankind*, Yuval Noah Harari discusses how ancient humans created myths to make sense of their world, stating, "Any large-scale human cooperation—whether a modern state, a medieval church, an ancient city, or an archaic tribe—is rooted in common myths that exist only in people's collective imagination" (Harari, 2015). These myths served a purpose in their time, but as our understanding of the world has evolved, these ancient narratives often fall short.

The logical inconsistencies and anachronistic views in religious doctrines become evident when contrasted with modern scientific discoveries. For instance, many religious explanations of creation are at odds with the Big Bang theory and the theory of evolution. Stephen Prothero, in *God is Not One*, highlights the divergent views among the world's major religions, emphasizing that these differences often stem from historical and cultural contexts rather than empirical truths (Prothero, 2010). As our knowledge of cosmology, biology and physics expands, the gap between scientific understanding and religious doctrine widens, making traditional religious explanations seem increasingly inadequate.

Furthermore, the moral and ethical guidelines proposed by ancient religions often clash with contemporary values and human rights. Issues such as gender equality, sexual orientation and individual freedom are approached very differently today compared to the times when these religious texts were written. Huston Smith's *The World's Religions* explores these differences, noting how the context in which a religion develops significantly influences its doctrines and practices. The evolution of societal norms and ethics challenges the applicability of ancient religious moral codes to modern life (Smith, 1991).

As our computational power and access to information have expanded, so has our understanding of the universe. This increased knowledge often leaves traditional religious explanations wanting. For instance, Neil Philip's *The Religions Book: Big Ideas Simply Explained* provides a comprehensive overview of world religions, yet it is evident that many of these beliefs were formulated in the pre-scientific era, lacking the nuanced understanding of reality that modern science provides. The rapid advancement of scientific knowledge has outpaced the ability of many religious doctrines to provide satisfactory explanations for contemporary issues (Philip, 2013).

The historical reliance on myth and storytelling as a means of explaining natural phenomena also contributes to the outdated nature of religious explanations. Carl Jung, in *The Undiscovered Self* discusses how mythological thinking shaped early human societies, yet he also acknowledges the limitations of these narratives in the face of scientific advancements. Jung suggests that while myths offer valuable insights into the human psyche, they must evolve to remain relevant. The transition from mythological to empirical explanations marks a significant shift in how humanity understands the world (Jung, 1957). More recently, Sabine Hossenfelder's *Existential Physics* underscores this point by exploring how modern physics challenges traditional notions of existence and reality. Hossenfelder argues that as our scientific understanding deepens, the explanatory power of religious narratives diminishes and the complex nature of quantum mechanics and the intricacies of the universe often stand in stark contrast to the simplistic explanations offered by many religious texts (Hossenfelder, 2022).

In this context, it becomes clear that traditional religions, while historically significant and culturally influential, struggle to provide satisfactory explanations for the core questions of existence. As Jobst

Landgrebe and Barry Smith discuss in *Why Machines Will Never Rule the World – On AI and Faith* (2021), the rapid advancements in artificial intelligence and computational power further highlight the limitations of religious doctrines rooted in ancient understandings of the world. The exponential growth in technological capabilities and scientific knowledge requires a foundation that can integrate these advancements without conflicting with established facts (Landgrebe and Smith, 2022).

Within this emerging paradigm The Simularity Proposition presents a framework that is difficult to dismiss. It offers an evidence-driven method for comprehending existence by merging knowledge with spiritual insights and acknowledges the limitations of beliefs while providing a more holistic interpretation of reality. By uniting evidence with experiences this integration fosters a comprehensive understanding of existence that resonates with both scientific inquiry and personal insight.

We are on the precipice of a seismic evolutionary paradigm shift where we are advancing to a new technology-instigated reality that impels us to shed the skin of obsolete belief systems that can no longer hold our species back from enlightened progress.

Viewing this next phase of our evolution as an element within a simulated framework can guide our approach to advancements in biology and technology. It urges us to reflect on the impacts of our choices and innovations acknowledging our role in an interconnected system. The very idea of The Simularity underscores how human evolution is a changing process. As we broaden our capabilities our perception of ourselves in relation to the universe also expands and deepens. This ongoing evolution challenges fixed doctrines that resist adaptation and change. The rapid progress in technology demands an agenda focused on incorporating new knowledge seamlessly without causing conflicts.

By combining insights from The Singularity and Simulation Hypothesis, The Simularity framework offers an approach to grappling with the intricacies of existence and consciousness. This holistic viewpoint provides an interpretation of reality encompassing both facts and spiritual encounters. The potential for an integrated comprehension of existence that melds data with wisdom marks a significant step forward in our exploration, for meaning and insight.

The Simularity Proposition underscores the significance of acknowledging and embracing knowledge and progress with logical reasoning in exploring existential inquiries.

PART FIVE

The Final Synthesis - Concluding Observations

The Simularity Proposition brings together two revolutionary ideas: The Singularity and The Simulation Hypothesis. Our exploration has shown that the merging of humans and technology is not a distant future event but a current reality. Innovation and exponential growth in computational power are bringing us to the seamless integration of biology and technology. These advancements and the many others we have explored within this essay indicate that The Singularity is unfolding now, reshaping our world in profound ways.

The Simulation Hypothesis posits that our reality could be a sophisticated simulation. This idea, once relegated to the realm of science fiction, has gained traction due to recent technological and scientific advancements. It offers a compelling and logical framework for understanding the universe and fits more coherently with our expanding knowledge of quantum physics and consciousness than many traditional theories.

The Simularity Proposition is the intersection of these two groundbreaking ideas. It suggests that as we approach The Singularity, our understanding of existence and reality will fundamentally change. This convergence will lead us to question the very nature of our universe and our place within it, offering new perspectives on age-old philosophical questions. It implies that we are on the cusp of a truly transformative paradigm shift in human thought and experience.

One of the core implications of The Simularity Proposition is the potential reshaping of religion and spirituality. Throughout history, religious beliefs have been a source of conflict and division among humans. The Simularity offers a new foundation for understanding our existence, one that transcends traditional religious and leap-of-faith boundaries. By providing a logical and scientific framework for concepts traditionally explained by religion, The Simularity could reduce conflicts rooted in religious differences and promote a more unified and progressive human experience inclusive of our innate spiritual inclinations.

Moreover, The Simularity Proposition opens possibilities for discovering new dimensions of existence. As our technological capabilities evolve, we may find ourselves capable of creating our own simulated realities or even multiverses. This ability would not only expand our understanding of the universe but also offer new opportunities for exploration and growth. The Simularity suggests that our quest for knowledge and understanding is far from over; instead, it is entering a new and exciting phase.

The future of human existence under The Simularity is one of limitless potential. As we continue to integrate technology into our lives and push the boundaries of what is possible, we will encounter new challenges and opportunities. The Simularity provides a framework for navigating this future, offering insights into how we can harness these advancements for the betterment of humanity. Understanding our place in the universe has always been the ultimate quest for humanity and The Simularity Proposition offers a new lens through which to view this quest. It suggests that our reality is part of a larger, more complex structure and one that we are only beginning to understand. This perspective encourages us to think beyond the limitations of our current knowledge and to embrace the possibilities of what lies ahead.

The potential economic and environmental benefits of The Simularity are significant. By reducing the need for scarce resources through advancements in biocomputing and other technologies we can mitigate environmental degradation and reduce conflicts over resources. This shift towards more sustainable technologies aligns with the broader goals of The Simularity, promoting a future where technology enhances rather than depletes our natural world.

This essay and its central theme is centered on the pursuit of knowledge and the expansion of human potential through the tools we create. It encourages us to explore the unknown and to embrace the challenges that come with it. The journey towards The Simularity is a collective one. It requires the collaboration of scientists, technologists, philosophers and thinkers from all walks of life. Together, we can build a future that reflects the best of what humanity has to offer, guided by the principles of curiosity, innovation and compassion.

The Simularity Proposition invites us to reimagine what is possible and to embrace the unknown with optimism and determination. It challenges us to think beyond the limitations of our current knowledge and to explore new frontiers of existence towards a future of boundless potential and discovery.

References

Aad, G., Abajyan, T., Abbott, B., Abdallah, J., Abdelalim, A. A., Abdinov, O., … & Collaboration, A. (2012). Observation of a new particle in the search for the Standard Model Higgs boson with the ATLAS detector at the LHC. *Physics Letters B, 716*(1), 1-29.

Aaronson, S. (2013). *Quantum Computing Since Democritus.* Cambridge University Press.

Ancient Sages. (2022, September 6). This universe existed before the big bang ft. Roger Penrose. *Medium.* https://medium.com/@ancientsages/this-universe-existed-before-the-big-bang-ft-roger-penrose-0325dba93fe3

Armstrong, K. (2009). *The Case for God: What Religion Really Means.* Alfred A. Knopf.

Arute, F., Arya, K., Babbush, R., Bacon, D., Bardin, J. C., Barends, R., … & Martinis, J. M. (2019). Quantum supremacy using a programmable superconducting processor. *Nature, 574*(7779), 505-510.

Aspect, A., Dalibard, J., & Roger, G. (1982). Experimental test of Bell's inequalities using time-varying analyzers. *Physical Review Letters, 49*(25), 1804-1807.

Barabási, A.-L. (2002). *Linked: How Everything Is Connected to Everything Else and What It Means.* Plume.

Baudrillard, J. (1994). *Simulacra and Simulation* (S. F. Glaser, Trans.). University of Michigan Press. (Original work published 1981)

BBC Science Focus. (2024). Something is wrong with our understanding of the Universe and the closer we look the weirder it gets. *BBC Science Focus Magazine.*

Bell, J. S. (1964). On the Einstein Podolsky Rosen Paradox. *Physics Physique Физика, 1*(3), 195-200.

Bennett, C. H., Brassard, G., Crépeau, C., Jozsa, R., Peres, A., & Zeilinger, A. (1993). Teleporting an unknown quantum state via dual classical and Einstein-Podolsky-Rosen channels. *Physical Review Letters, 70*(13), 1895-1899.

Bennett, C. L., Halpern, M., Hinshaw, G., Jarosik, N., Kogut, A., Limon, M., ... & Wright, E. L. (2003). First-year Wilkinson Microwave Anisotropy Probe (WMAP) observations: Preliminary maps and basic results. *The Astrophysical Journal Supplement Series*, 148*(1), 1-27.

Berkeley, G. (1710). A Treatise Concerning the Principles of Human Knowledge.

Big Think. (2023). How quantum computing could change everything everywhere. *Big Think*. Retrieved from https://www.bigthink.com

Blackmore, S. (2005). *Consciousness: A Very Short Introduction*. Oxford University Press.

Bohr, N. (1913). On the constitution of atoms and molecules. *Philosophical Magazine*, 26*(153), 1-25.

Bohm, D. (1980). *Wholeness and the Implicate Order*. Routledge & Kegan Paul.

Bostrom, N. (2003). Are you living in a Computer simulation? *Philosophical Quarterly*, 53*(211), 243-255.

Bostrom, N. (2005). Transhumanist values. *Journal of Philosophical Research*, 30*(Supplement), 3-14.

Bostrom, N. (2014). *Superintelligence: Paths, Dangers, Strategies*. Oxford University Press.

Bostrom, N., & Yudkowsky, E. (2014). The ethics of artificial intelligence. In K. Frankish & W. M. Ramsey (Eds.), *The Cambridge Handbook of Artificial Intelligence* (pp. 316-334). Cambridge University Press.

Brynjolfsson, E., & McAfee, A. (2011). *Race Against the Machine: How the Digital Revolution is Accelerating Innovation, Driving Productivity, and Irreversibly Transforming Employment and the Economy*. Digital Frontier Press.

Brynjolfsson, E., & McAfee, A. (2014). *The Second Machine Age: Work, Progress, and Prosperity in a Time of Brilliant Technologies*. W.W. Norton & Company.

Carrasquilla, J., & Melko, R. G. (2017). Machine learning phases of matter. *Nature Physics*, 13*(5), 431-434.

Cassirer, E. (1951). *The Philosophy of the Enlightenment.* Princeton University Press.

Chalmers, D.J. (1996). *The Conscious Mind: In Search of a Fundamental Theory.* Oxford University Press.

Chalmers, D. J. (2003). The Matrix as Metaphysics. In C. Grau (Ed.), *Philosophers Explore The Matrix* (pp. 132-176). Oxford University Press.

Chalmers, D. J. (2010). *The Character of Consciousness.* Oxford University Press.

Chalmers, D. J. (2016). The Virtual and the Real. *Disputatio,* 8*(42), 309-352.

Christian, D. (2004). *Maps of Time: An Introduction to Big History.* University of California Press.

Clark, A. (2003). *Natural-Born Cyborgs: Minds, Technologies, and the Future of Human Intelligence.* Oxford University Press.

Copernicus, N. (1543). *On the Revolutions of the Heavenly Spheres.*

Crawford, K. (2021). *Atlas of AI: Power, Politics, and the Planetary Costs of Artificial Intelligence.* Yale University Press.

d'Aquili, E. G., & Newberg, A. B. (1999). *The Mystical Mind: Probing the Biology of Religious Experience.* Fortress Press.

Darwin, C. (1859). *On the Origin of Species by Means of Natural Selection.* John Murray.

Davies, P. C. W., & Brown, J. R. (Eds.). (1986). *The Ghost in the Atom: A Discussion of the Mysteries of Quantum Physics.* Cambridge University Press.

Dawkins, R. (2006). *The God Delusion.* Houghton Mifflin.

Dennett, D. C. (1996). *Kinds of Minds: Toward an Understanding of Consciousness.* Basic Books.

Deutsch, D. (1997). *The Fabric of Reality: The Science of Parallel Universes— and its Implications.* Penguin Books.

Diamandis, P. (2011). The future according to Ray Kurzweil. Retrieved from https://www.kurzweilai.net/the-future-according-to-ray-kurzweil

Doudna, J. A., & Charpentier, E. (2014). The new frontier of genome engineering with CRISPR-Cas9. *Science, 346**(6213).

Drexler, K. E. (1992). *Nanosystems: Molecular Machinery, Manufacturing, and Computation.* John Wiley & Sons.

Eagleman, D. (2011). *Incognito: The Secret Lives of the Brain.* Pantheon Books.

Eagleman, D. (2015). *The Brain: The Story of You.* Pantheon Books.

Einstein, A. (1905). Concerning an heuristic point of view toward the emission and transformation of light. *Annalen der Physik, 17*,* 132-148.

Einstein, A. (1916). *Relativity: The Special and the General Theory.* H. Holt and Company.

Einstein, A. (1916). The Foundation of the General Theory of Relativity. *Annalen der Physik, 49*,* 769-822.

Endy, D. (2005). Foundations for engineering biology. *Nature, 438**(7067), 449-453.

Evans, R. J. (2018). *Altered Pasts: Counterfactuals in History.* Brandeis University Press.

Everett, H. (1957). "Relative State" Formulation of Quantum Mechanics. *Reviews of Modern Physics, 29**(3), 454-462. https://doi.org/10.1103/RevModPhys.29.454

Feynman, R. P. (1982). Simulating physics with computers. *International Journal of Theoretical Physics, 21**(6-7), 467-488.

Floridi, L. (2010). *Information: A Very Short Introduction.* Oxford University Press.

Floridi, L. (2014). *The Fourth Revolution: How the Infosphere is Reshaping Human Reality.* Oxford University Press.

Fisher, M. P. A. (2015). Quantum cognition: The possibility of processing with nuclear spins in the brain. *Annals of Physics, 362*,* 593-602. https://doi.org/10.1016/j.aop.2015.08.020

Friston, K. J. (2010). The free-energy principle: a unified brain theory? *Nature Reviews Neuroscience, 11**(2), 127-138.

Fredriksson, I. (2018). *Essays on Physics, Death and the Mind.* Springer.

GeekWire. (2023). Quantum Supremacy: How the Quantum Computer Revolution Will Change Everything. *GeekWire.* Retrieved from https://www.geekwire.com

Geim, A. K., & Novoselov, K. S. (2007). The rise of graphene. *Nature Materials, 6*(3), 183-191.

Goff, P. (2019). *Galileo's Error: Foundations for a New Science of Consciousness.* Pantheon Books.

Goodall, N. J. (2014). Machine ethics and automated vehicles. In *Road Vehicle Automation* (pp. 93-102).

Goody, J. (1987). *The Interface Between the Written and the Oral.* Cambridge University Press.

Gough, E. (2020). Could the universe be a simulation? Scientists debate in new AI-driven research. *Scientific American.* Retrieved from https://www.scientificamerican.com/article/could-the-universe-be-a-simulation-scientists-debate-in-new-ai-driven-research/

Gould, S. J. (1997). *Nonoverlapping Magisteria.* Natural History, 106(2), 16-22.

Greene, B. (2005). *The Fabric of the Cosmos: Space, Time, and the Texture of Reality.* Penguin Books.

Greyson, B. (2003). Incidence and correlates of near-death experiences in a cardiac care unit. *General Hospital Psychiatry, 25*(4), 269-276.

Grey, D. B. (2020). *Quantum Physics for Beginners Who Flunked Math and Science: Quantum Mechanics and Physics Made Easy Guide in Plain Simple English.* Bluesource And Friends.

Guth, A. H. (1981). Inflationary universe: A possible solution to the horizon and flatness problems. *Physical Review D, 23*(2), 347-356.

Hameroff, S. & Penrose, R. (2014). Consciousness in the universe: A review of the 'Orch OR' theory. *Physics of Life Reviews, 11*(1), 39-78.

Hanson, R. (2016). *The Age of Em: Work, Love, and Life when Robots Rule the Earth.* Oxford University Press.

Harari, Y. N. (2015). *Sapiens: A Brief History of Humankind*. Harper.

Harari, Y. N. (2016). *Homo Deus: A Brief History of Tomorrow*. Harper.

Harris, J. (2007). *Enhancing Evolution: The Ethical Case for Making Better People*. Princeton University Press.

Harris, S. (2004). *The End of Faith: Religion, Terror, and the Future of Reason*. W.W. Norton & Company.

Hawking, S. (1988). *A Brief History of Time*. Bantam Books.

Heisenberg, W. (1927). Über den anschaulichen Inhalt der quantentheoretischen Kinematik und Mechanik. *Zeitschrift für Physik*, 43*(3-4), 172-198.

Hoffman, D. (2023). New Evidence For The Simulation Hypothesis? Donald Hoffman on The Simulation Argument [Video]. YouTube. https://www.youtube.com/watch?v=RhAgpq26Noc

Hofstadter, D. R. (2007). *I Am a Strange Loop*. Basic Books.

Horgan, J. (2018). Mind-Body Problems: Science, Subjectivity, & Who We Really Are. *Lulu.com*.

Hornung, E. (1999). *The Ancient Egyptian Books of the Afterlife*. Cornell University Press.

Horodecki, R., Horodecki, P., Horodecki, M., & Horodecki, K. (2009). Quantum entanglement. *Reviews of Modern Physics*, 81*(2), 865-942.

Hossenfelder, S. (2022). *Existential Physics: A Scientist's Guide to Life's Biggest Questions*. Basic Books.

Hubble, E. (1929). A relation between distance and radial velocity among extra-galactic nebulae. *Proceedings of the National Academy of Sciences*, 15*(3), 168-173.

Hughes, J. (2004). *Citizen Cyborg: Why Democratic Societies Must Respond to the Redesigned Human of the Future*. Westview Press.

Husserl, E. (1913). Ideas: General introduction to pure phenomenology.

Huxley, J. (1942). *Evolution: The Modern Synthesis*. Harper & Brothers.

Jaynes, J. (1976). *The Origin of Consciousness in the Breakdown of the Bicameral Mind*. Houghton Mifflin.

Jeans, J. (1930). *The Mysterious Universe*. Cambridge University Press.

Jung, C. G. (1957). *The Undiscovered Self*. Routledge.

Jung, C. G. (1961). *Memories, Dreams, Reflections*. Pantheon Books.

Kafatos, M., & Nadeau, R. (2000). *The Conscious Universe: Parts and Wholes in Physical Reality*. Springer.

Kaku, M. (2014). *The Future of the Mind: The Scientific Quest to Understand, Enhance, and Empower the Mind*. Doubleday.

Kaku, M. (2021). *The God Equation: The Quest for a Theory of Everything*. Doubleday.

Kelly, K. (2005). Ray Kurzweil's mind-boggling predictions. *Wired*. Retrieved from https://www.wired.com/2005/12/kurzweil/

Kelly, K. (2010). *What Technology Wants*. Viking.

Kelly, K. (2016). *The Inevitable: Understanding the 12 Technological Forces That Will Shape Our Future*. Viking.

Kirk, G. S. (1974). *The Nature of Greek Myths*. Penguin Books.

Klein, J. T. (1990). *Interdisciplinarity: History, Theory, and Practice*. Wayne State University Press.

Kuhn, T. S. (1957). *The Copernican Revolution: Planetary Astronomy in the Development of Western Thought*. Harvard University Press.

Kurzweil, R. (2001). The Law of Accelerating Returns. Retrieved from https://www.kurzweilai.net/the-law-of-accelerating-returns

Kurzweil, R. (2005). *The Singularity Is Near: When Humans Transcend Biology*. Viking.

Kurzweil, R. (2012). *How to Create a Mind: The Secret of Human Thought Revealed*. Viking.

Landgrebe, J., & Smith, B. (2022). *Why Machines Will Never Rule the World: Artificial Intelligence Without Fear*. Routledge.

Lanier, J. (2010). *You Are Not a Gadget: A Manifesto*. Knopf.

Lanier, J. (2017). *Dawn of the New Everything: Encounters with Reality and Virtual Reality*. Henry Holt and Co.

Lebedev, M. A., & Nicolelis, M. A. L. (2006). Brain–machine interfaces: Past, present and future. *Trends in Neurosciences, 29*(9), 536-546.

LeCun, Y. (2019). Learning from experience and the future of AI. *Journal of Machine Learning Research*, 20(1), 1-30.

LeCun, Y., Bengio, Y., & Hinton, G. (2015). Deep learning. *Nature, 521*(7553), 436-444. https://doi.org/10.1038/nature14539

Lin, P. (2013). Ethics of Human Enhancement in the Military. In J. Forge (Ed.), *The Military and Ethics*. Springer.

Lloyd, S. (2006). *Programming the Universe: A Quantum Computer Scientist Takes on the Cosmos*. Knopf.

Marcus, G. (2018). The Trouble with AI. *The New Yorker*. Retrieved from https://www.newyorker.com/tech/elements/the-trouble-with-ai

Maynard Smith, J. (1999). *The Origins of Life: From the Birth of Life to the Origin of Language*. Oxford University Press.

Mayr, E. (1982). *The Growth of Biological Thought: Diversity, Evolution, and Inheritance*. Belknap Press.

McLuhan, M. (1964). *Understanding Media: The Extensions of Man*. McGraw-Hill.

Metzinger, T. (2009). *The Ego Tunnel: The Science of the Mind and the Myth of the Self*. Basic Books.

Moore, G. E. (1965). Cramming more components onto integrated circuits. *Electronics, 38*(8).

Moravec, H. (1988). *Mind Children: The Future of Robot and Human Intelligence*. Harvard University Press.

More, M. (2013). The Philosophy of Transhumanism. In M. More & N. Vita-More (Eds.), *The Transhumanist Reader: Classical and Contemporary Essays on the Science, Technology, and Philosophy of the Human Future*. Wiley-Blackwell.

Musk, E. (2017). Neuralink and the Brain's Magical Future. Wait But Why. Retrieved from https://waitbutwhy.com/2017/04/neuralink.html

Musk, E. (2020). Neuralink progress update, Summer 2020. Retrieved from https://www.neuralink.com/

Musser, G. (2015). *Spooky Action at a Distance: The Phenomenon that Reimagines Space and Time—and What It Means for Black Holes, the Big Bang, and Theories of Everything.* Farrar, Straus and Giroux.

Musser, G. (2021). Incorporating ourselves into the equation: How physicists are investigating human consciousness and AI to unravel the universe's mysteries. *Scientific American, 325*(4), 24-33.

National Human Genome Research Institute. (2020). The Cost of Sequencing a Human Genome. Retrieved from https://www.genome.gov/about-genomics/fact-sheets/Sequencing-Human-Genome-cost

Neumann, E. (1954*). The Origins and History of Consciousness.* Princeton University Press.

Neural Networks. (2022, December 14). The terrifying quantum theory scientists don't even want to talk about [Video]. YouTube. https://www.youtube.com/watch?v=IvD9MOiHsx8

Newberg, A., & Waldman, M. R. (2009). *How God Changes Your Brain: Breakthrough Findings from a Leading Neuroscientist.* Ballantine Books.

Newton, I. (1999). *The Principia: Mathematical Principles of Natural Philosophy* (I. B. Cohen & A. Whitman, Trans.). University of California Press. (Original work published 1687).

Nietzsche, F. (1883). *Thus Spoke Zarathustra: A Book for All and None.*

Nielsen, M. A., & Chuang, I. L. (2010). *Quantum Computation and Quantum Information: 10th Anniversary Edition.* Cambridge University Press.

Nussbaum, M. C. (2001*). Upheavals of Thought: The Intelligence of Emotions.* Cambridge University Press.

Olson, C. (2007). *The Many Colors of Hinduism: A Thematic-Historical Introduction.* Rutgers University Press.

Parfit, D. (1984). *Reasons and Persons.* Oxford University Press.

Parnia, S. (2013). *Erasing Death: The Science That is Rewriting the Boundaries Between Life and Death*. HarperOne.

Penrose, R. (1989). *The Emperor's New Mind: Concerning Computers, Minds, and the Laws of Physics*. Oxford University Press.

Perez, C. (2002). *Technological Revolutions and Financial Capital: The Dynamics of Bubbles and Golden Ages*. Edward Elgar Publishing.

Philip, N. (2013). *The Religions Book: Big Ideas Simply Explained*. DK.

Planck, M. (1901). Ueber das Gesetz der Energieverteilung im Normalspectrum. *Annalen der Physik*, 4*(10), 553-563.

Plato. (2007). *The Republic*. Penguin Classics. (Original work published ca. 380 BCE)

Popper, K. (1959). *The Logic of Scientific Discovery*. Routledge.

Prothero, S. (2010). *God is Not One: The Eight Rival Religions That Run the World*. HarperOne.

Putnam, H. (1981). *Reason, Truth, and History*. Cambridge University Press.

Rojas, R., & Hashagen, U. (2000). *The First Computers: History and Architectures*. MIT Press.

Russell, S. (2019). *Human Compatible: Artificial Intelligence and the Problem of Control*. Viking.

Russell, S., & Norvig, P. (2020). *Artificial Intelligence: A Modern Approach* (4th ed.). Pearson.

Sartre, J-P. (1946). *Existentialism is a Humanism* (P. Mairet, Trans.). Methuen.

Savulescu, J. (2009). *Enhancing Human Capacities*. Wiley-Blackwell.

Savulescu, J. (2011). *Unfit for the Future: The Need for Moral Enhancement*. Oxford University Press.

Searle, J. (1980). Minds, brains, and programs. *Behavioral and Brain Sciences*, 3*(3), 417-424.

Seth, A. (2021). *Being You: A New Science of Consciousness*. Dutton.

Schmidt, A., Kroll, J., Barnes, C., Buhler, K., & Bischof, H. (2017). Climate simulation with machine learning: An empirical evaluation. *International Conference on Learning Representations (ICLR)*. Retrieved from https://arxiv.org/abs/1707.00140

Schneider, S. (2019). *Artificial You: AI and the Future of Your Mind*. Princeton University Press.

Schrödinger, E. (1935). Discussion of probability relations between separated systems. *Mathematical Proceedings of the Cambridge Philosophical Society*, 31*(4), 555-563.

Sejnowski, T. J. (2020). *The Deep Learning Revolution*. MIT Press.

Sheldrake, R. (2013). Exposing Scientific Dogmas - Banned TED Talk - Rupert Sheldrake [Video]. YouTube. https://www.youtube.com/watch?v=sF03FN37i5w&list=PLByyA8H1xDpwD6l25aB-ef3IteBz-wFeT&index=7

Shor, P. W. (1994). Algorithms for quantum computation: Discrete logarithms and factoring. In *Proceedings 35th Annual Symposium on Foundations of Computer Science* (pp. 124-134). IEEE.

Silver, D., et al. (2016). Mastering the game of Go with deep neural networks and tree search. *Nature*, 529*(7587), 484-489.

Smith, H. (1991). *The World's Religions: Our Great Wisdom Traditions*. HarperOne.

Smoot, G. (2019). YouTube video. "Are we living in a simulation? | Nobel Prize winner George Smoot."

Sobel, D. (2011). *A More Perfect Heaven: How Copernicus Revolutionized the Cosmos*. Bloomsbury Publishing.

Stapp, H. P. (2017). *Quantum Theory and Free Will: How Mental Intentions Translate into Bodily Actions*. Springer.

Swade, D. (2000). *The Difference Engine: Charles Babbage and the Quest to Build the First Computer*. Penguin Books.

Susskind, L. (2008). *The Black Hole War: My Battle with Stephen Hawking to Make the World Safe for Quantum Mechanics*. Little, Brown.

Susskind, R. (2020). *Online Courts and the Future of Justice.* Oxford University Press.

Tegmark, M. (2003). Parallel universes. *Scientific American*, 288*(5), 40-51.

Tegmark, M. (2008). The Mathematical Universe. *Foundations of Physics*, 38*(2), 101-150.

Tegmark, M. (2014*). Our Mathematical Universe: My Quest for the Ultimate Nature of Reality.* Knopf.

Tegmark, M. (2018). *Life 3.0: Being Human in the Age of Artificial Intelligence.* Knopf.

Tononi, G. (2008). Consciousness as Integrated Information: A Provisional Manifesto. *The Biological Bulletin*, 215*(3), 216-242.

Tononi, G. (2015). Integrated information theory. *Schizophrenia Bulletin*, 41*(4), 911-912.

Topol, E. (2019). *Deep Medicine: How Artificial Intelligence Can Make Healthcare Human Again.* Basic Books.

Turkle, S. (2011). *Alone Together: Why We Expect More from Technology and Less from Each Other.* Basic Books.

Turing, A. M. (1950). Computing machinery and intelligence. *Mind*, 59*(236), 433-460.

Tyson, M. (2024). World's first bioprocessor uses 16 human brain organoids for 'a million times less power' consumption than a digital chip. *Tom's Hardware*. Retrieved from Tom's Hardware.

Vedral, V. (2010). *Decoding Reality: The Universe as Quantum Information.* Oxford University Press.

Vinge, V. (1993). The Coming Technological Singularity: How to Survive in the Post-Human Era. In *Vision-21: Interdisciplinary Science and Engineering in the Era of Cyberspace* (pp. 11-22). NASA.

Virk, R. (2019). *The Simulation Hypothesis: An MIT Computer Scientist Shows Why AI, Quantum Physics and Eastern Mystics All Agree We Are in a Video Game.* Bayview Books.

Virk, R. (2021). *The Simulated Multiverse: An MIT Computer Scientist Explores Parallel Universes, the Simulation Hypothesis, Quantum Computing, and the Mandela Effect*. Bayview Books.

Vita-More, N. (2015). The prosthetic aesthetic: A case for a posthumanist transhumanism. In E. Parry & J. E. Downing (Eds.), *The Palgrave Handbook of Posthumanism in Film and Television* (pp. 165-172). Palgrave Macmillan.

Wade, J. (1996). *Changes of Mind: A Holonomic Theory of the Evolution of Consciousness*. SUNY Press.

Wallach, W., & Allen, C. (2009). *Moral Machines: Teaching Robots Right from Wrong*. Oxford University Press.

West, G. (2017). *Scale: The Universal Laws of Growth, Innovation, Sustainability, and the Pace of Life in Organisms, Cities, Economies, and Companies*. Penguin Press.

Westfall, R. S. (1971). *The Construction of Modern Science: Mechanisms and Mechanics*. Cambridge University Press.

Wheeler, J. A. (1978). The "Past" and the "Delayed-Choice" Double-Slit Experiment. *Mathematical Foundations of Quantum Theory*, 9*, 48-51.

Wheeler, J. A. (1990). Information, Physics, Quantum: The Search for Links. In Zurek, W. H. (Ed.), *Complexity, Entropy, and the Physics of Information*. Addison-Wesley.

Wilson, E. O. (2002). *The Future of Life*. Vintage.

Zeilinger, A. (2010). *Dance of the Photons: From Einstein to Quantum Teleportation*. Farrar, Straus and Giroux.

Zhuangzi. (369-286 BCE). *The Complete Works of Zhuangzi*. Translated by Burton Watson. Columbia University Press.

Zuboff, S. (2019). *The Age of Surveillance Capitalism: The Fight for a Human Future at the New Frontier of Power*. PublicAffairs.